Volume 1

make it yourself

The Complete Step-by-Step Library of Needlework and Crafts

COLUMBIA HOUSE/New York

Editor: Mary Harding
Assistant Editor: Margo Coughtrie
Editorial Assistant: Sally Fisher
Consultants: Greta Barrett/Angela Jeffs (Sewing)/
Patsy North (Embroidery and Crafts)/
Frances Rogers (Knitting and Crochet)
Managing Editor: Nicholas Wright
Design Co-ordinators: David Harper/Jan Browne
Production Control: Frank Sloan
Editorial Director: Graham Donaldson

Distributed by Columbia House, 51 West 52nd Street, New York, New York 10019

Contents

How to use this book...

Selecting a yarn

In this series, we are introducing a new and easy way to identify the yarn used in our knitting and crochet features! You will find an actual-size, colored photograph of the yarn given with each set of directions.

Materials Required:

150 (200) gm or 6 (7) oz each of yellow and green, 50 gm or 2 oz blue [100 gm = 360 m or 390 yds]. Knitting needles size 4 (Am) or 10 (Eng).

At one time or another, you have probably suffered the disappointment of finding that the yarn specified in knitting and crochet directions is difficult to obtain or totally unavailable in your area. When this happens you are faced with the often impossible task of finding a substitute yarn. By matching a yarn against our photograph, you can choose a yarn of similar weight and texture from the range of yarns available in your store or favorite needlework shop.

This method is also helpful if you have yarn left over from other projects and you are unsure whether it is the proper weight or texture and whether you have sufficient yardage to finish a new shawl or pullover.

To help you determine the amount of yarn needed, we have also listed the yardage per skein for the yarn used. Most yarn companies give the yardage per skein in their sample books, and many shops have interchangeable yarn lists which give the yardages per unit weight. You will then be able to see whether you will need to make adjustments in the number of skeins required of the yarn which you have chosen.

Before you start to work the patter work a test swatch and match against the Tension given in t directions (see the Tension Gau instructions below). Adjust t needle or hook size if necessar Any yarn which can be worked the tension given in the directio can be used for that pattern.

Centimeters or inches?

The metric system of measureme is gaining greater use and accep ance, and some needlework ar crafts equipment and materials a already sold by the metric weig and/or length. For your co venience, we have given all th weights and measures in bot systems. NOTE: In some cases, th conversions are not exact. Th measurements have been rounde to the nearest convenient o appropriate number.

Tension gauge

One key to successful knitting or crocheting is the tension! Each of our directions is based on the given tension gauge (number of rows and stitches to 10 cm or 4″).

To check your tension, work a test piece 12 cm or 5″ square in the stitch pattern. Make a cardboard template with a 10 cm or 4″ square cut out of it. Place the template over your swatch and count the rows and stitches. Compare the numbers with the tension gauge given in the directions. If your swatch has too few stitches and rows, work more tightly or use smaller equipment. If you have more than the number given, use larger needles, or hook. Directions for the items shown can be used for any yarn of similar thickness and texture, providing you can achieve the proper tension.

Do not be upset if you find that you do have to adjust the needle or hook size. This does not mean that there is anything wrong with your knitting or crocheting. The needle and hook sizes given in the directions are an average, but by no means an absolute. There is great variation in the tension at which different people work, and you will even find slight variations in the tension of your work. On days when you are tens or tired, your knitting or crochetin will probably be a little tighter.

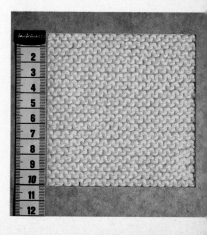

ashion sizing

essmaking

› you know your size? Don't just · 'yes', because as you already ow, the fit of pattern and ready- ·wear sizes varies.

› eliminate confusion, we have tered our sizes (A, B, C) instead giving them the traditional mbering (10, 12).

:measure yourself and match your· ›dy measurements with those ven in the chart below. All of the tterns are designed according to ese measurements, so choose the ttern size which is right for your easurements. You may have to ake minor adjustments in the ttern pieces to adapt them to ›ur body contours, and Dress- aking Pattern Sheet 2 explains ›w to do this. Other dressmaking ttern sheets will deal with more ›mplex fitting for specific garments ch as pants.

O NOT MEASURE THE ATTERNS. Every pattern includes, cording to the design, an added easure to allow for easy movement hen wearing the garment. Just ›mpare your body measurements ith the measurements given in the art and choose the proper size.

ach pattern is given in five sizes. wo of the sizes are given on the attern sheet and the other three zes can be easily drawn from the two sizes given. Directions for adapting for the three additional sizes are given on each pattern sheet. Even if you are not one of the standard pattern sizes, but are a mixed size made up of several standard measurements, you can still use our patterns. Since each pattern can be adapted for five sizes – a size smaller, a size larger, and a size between the two sizes actually marked on the pattern sheet – it is possible to construct a pattern for yourself. Directions for constructing a mixed-size pattern are given on Dressmaking Pattern Sheet 2.

Knitting and Crochet

The knitting and crochet sizes are based on the Dressmaking Body Measurements Chart. For each direction, you will be given the actual body measurements for which the garment is intended. The finished knitted or crocheted garment will be larger than the given measurements to allow for comfort and movement.

Size: Directions are for 92 cm (36″) bust. Changes for 96, 100 cm (37½″, 39½″) bust are in brackets.

Do you know your size?

Don't just say 'yes'. Remeasure yourself, following the diagrams and instructions, and then check the Body Measurements chart.

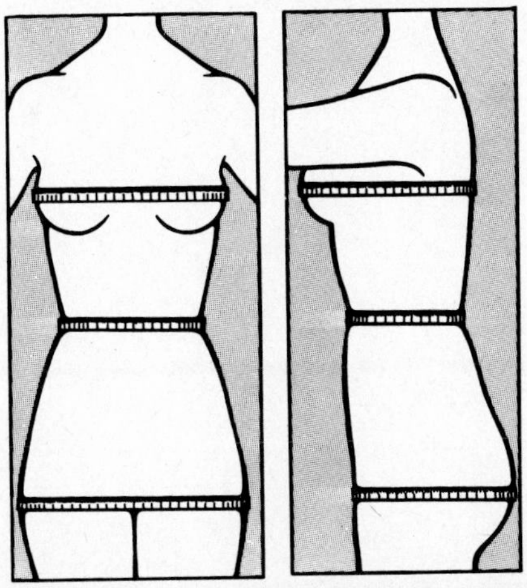

Bust – measure around the fullest part of the bust.

Waist – tie a string around your body so that it settles comfortably at your natural waistline. Measure your waist at the string.

Hips – measure around the fullest part of your hips (this generally falls 7″–9″ below your waistline).

Important hints:

When taking measurements, do not hold the tape measure slack or pull it too tight. The tape must lie evenly horizontal all around the body – it should not go up at the back and down at the front. You will find it simpler and more accurate to be measured by someone else.

Body measurements chart

VOMEN

Size	A	B	C	D	E	F	G	H
Bust	80 cm (31½″)	84 cm (33″)	88 cm (34½″)	92 cm (36″)	96 cm (37½″)	100 cm (39½″)	104 cm (41″)	108 cm (42½″)
Waist	59 cm (23¼″)	63.5 cm (25″)	68 cm (26½″)	72.5 cm (28½″)	77 cm (30½″)	81.5 cm (32″)	86 cm (34″)	90 cm (35½″)
Hips	86 cm (34″)	90 cm (35½″)	94 cm (37″)	98 cm (38½″)	102 cm (40″)	106 cm (42″)	110 cm (43½″)	114 cm (45″)

ΛEN

Size	J	K	L	M	N	O	P	Q
Chest	84 cm (33″)	88 cm (34½″)	92 cm (36″)	96 cm (37½″)	100 cm (39½″)	104 cm (41″)	108 cm (42½″)	112 cm (44″)
Hip	88 cm (34½″)	92 cm (36″)	96 cm (37½″)	100 cm (39½″)	104 cm (41″)	108 cm (42½″)	112 cm (44″)	116 cm (45½″)
Neck	36 cm (14″)	37 cm (14½″)	38 cm (15″)	39 cm (15½″)	40 cm (15¾″)	41 cm (16″)	42 cm (16½″)	43 cm (17″)
Arm	60 cm (23¾″)	61 cm (24″)	62 cm (24¼″)	63 cm (24¾″)	64 cm (25¼″)	65 cm (25½″)	66 cm (26″)	67 cm (26½″)

:HILDREN

Size	S	T	U	V	W	X	Y	Z
Height	110 cm (43″)	116 cm (45½″)	122 cm (48″)	128 cm (50½″)	134 cm (52¾″)	140 cm (55″)	146 cm (57½″)	152 cm (60″)
Chest	60 cm (23¾″)	62 cm (24¼″)	64 cm (25¼″)	66 cm (26″)	68 cm (26¾″)	70 cm (27½″)	73 cm (28¾″)	76 cm (29¾″)
Waist	58 cm (23″)	59 cm (23¼″)	60 cm (23¾″)	61 cm (24″)	62 cm (24¼″)	63 cm (24¾″)	64 cm (25¼″)	65 cm (25¾″)
Hips	66 cm (26″)	68 cm (26¾″)	70 cm (27½″)	72 cm (28¼″)	74 cm (29″)	76 cm (29¾″)	80 cm (31½″)	84 cm (33″)

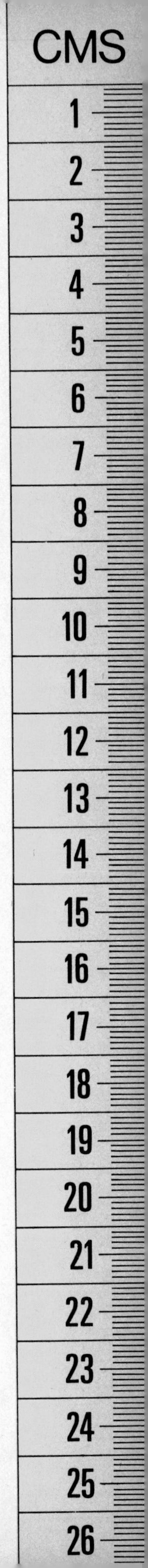

make it yourself

Introduction

This series is for people who value traditional hand-crafted methods and creative self-satisfaction, but who want projects which are filled with imagination, style, and fun . . . as well as love.

One of the first questions you are bound to ask yourself when a new needlework and crafts library appears is, "What's different about it?" *Make It Yourself* is different—in its approach, in its attitude, in its contents and presentation.

We have two main aims. The first is to convince every woman that it doesn't take an artist or a professional to make all the lovely things pictured inside. The second is to give that professional touch to the woman who doesn't want her finished designs to look "homemade."

To fit in with your busy life, we've taken special care to introduce helpful working aids. We've made the instructions clear and concise and illustrated each technique with step-by-step colored photographs which can be used as lessons by beginners or for review by the more experienced.

We explain the *why* as well as the *how* so that you will not only be able to enjoy making the many items in the book, but you will be able to use these projects as

(continued)

a starting point for exploring the creative potential of needlework and crafts. And where there is a short cut which won't jeopardize the end result, we tell you how to do it.

To eliminate the guesswork when buying yarns, we've given an actual-size photograph of the yarn used for each knitting and crochet feature. You can see exactly what the yarn looks like, so rather than searching for a specific yarn, you can use any yarn of similar weight and texture (see Tension Gauge, page 4).

The series builds into a family library of specially designed projects for all levels of skill and experience in knitting, crochet, sewing, embroidery, canvaswork, rugmaking, beading, weaving, macramé, leather-craft, and paper craft.

Volume by volume, *Make It Yourself* gives you a wide range of distinctive fashions and accessories, plus countless ideas which will add a unique and personal touch to your home decorating.

Together, these new and exciting projects will provide you and your family with many hours of creative pleasure and satisfaction.

The top story in stripes

ze: Directions are for
cm (36") bust. Changes
r 96, 100 cm (37½",
") bust are in brackets.

aterials Required:

50 (200) gm or 6 (7) oz
ch white, green; 50 gm
2 oz blue [100 gm =
50 m or 390 yds]. Knitting
edles size 4 (Am) or 10
ng). Stitch holder.

asic Stitch: Garter Stitch
nit every row).

olor Sequence 1: Knit 3
ws blue, 2 rows white, 8
ws green, 2 rows white,
rows blue.

olor Sequence 2: Knit
rows white, 2 rows green.

ension: 23 stitches and
rows = 10 cm or 4".

RECTIONS

ack: Cast on 110 (114:
20) stitches in blue. Work
olor Sequence 1 and knit
stitches together at each
nd of 10th row.
Vork Color Sequence 2 and
ecrease 1 stitch at each
nd of 1st row, then every
0th row 3 times — 100
04:110) stitches. Work
raight until piece measures
7 cm or 6¾".
crease 1 stitch at each
nd of next row, then every
4th row 4 times more —
10 (114:120) stitches.
Vork straight until back
easures 33 cm or 13".
hape Armholes: Cast off 5
5:8) stitches at beginning
f next 2 rows, 3 (4:5)
itches next 2 rows, 2
itches next 4 rows.
ecrease 1 stitch at each
nd of next 2 rows, then
very 4th row twice — 78
itches. Work straight until
ack measures 52 (53:53)

Here is a good-looking
striped pullover made
in simple garter stitch.
Don't worry about
trying a v-neck – this
border is knitted
separately and
sewn on. Easy!

cm or 20½″ (21″:21″).

Shape Shoulders: Cast off 3 stitches at each armhole edge every other row 6 times. *At the same time,* 4 rows above the beginning of shoulder decrease, cast off center 32 stitches for neck edge. Place one shoulder on stitch holder. Continuing armhole decrease every other row at neck edge, cast off 2 stitches twice and 1 stitch once. Repeat for other shoulder.

Front: Work as for back except for neck decrease. Begin working V-neck decrease 4 rows before armhole decrease. Divide work and place half the stitches on a stitch holder. Decrease 1 stitch at neck edge every other row 9 times, 1 stitch every 4th row 8. times, then 1 stitch every 6th row 4 times. Repeat for other half.

Neck Border: Cast on 156 stitches in blue. Work Color Sequence 1, decreasing 1 stitch at each end of every row. Cast off.

Armhole Border: For each, cast on 100 (102:106) stitches in blue; knit 4 rows. Cast off.

Finishing: Sew front and back together, being careful to match colors. Sew on neck and armhole borders.

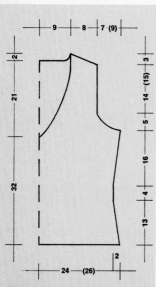

Half-pattern for the smallest (largest) sizes. The numbers are given in centimeters.

Casting on
Knitting, Casting off
Tension gaug

Casting On

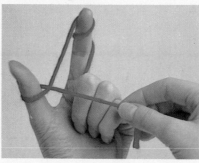

1 Wind the measured length of yarn around index finger of your left hand and once around thumb.

4 After you have drawn the stra through the loop with the need remove your thumb from the loop.

2 Grasp both strands in your left hand; insert both needles up through bottom of the thumb loop.

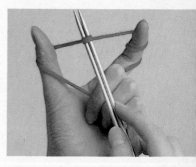

5 Pull strands with thumb and ind finger until knot is close to need forming first stitch as shown.

3 Pass the needles from right to left behind strand of yarn on index finger. Pull yarn down through the thumb loop with the pair of needles.

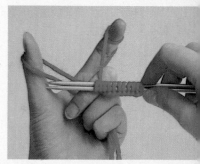

6 The yarn is around thumb a ready for the next stitch. Repeat ste 2–5 for required number of stitch Remove one needle to begin knitting.

l knitting begins with a cast-on edge. To determine the
mount of yarn needed for casting on, allow 1cm ($\frac{1}{2}$″) for each
tch when using lightweight yarn. For thicker yarn, allow
m (1″) per stitch, plus 20 cm (8″). When using lightweight
medium-weight yarn, cast on with two needles for a more
astic edge. All knitting ends with a cast-off edge.

nitting

Always keep yarn behind work.
sert right needle into first stitch on
t needle from left to right.

Right needle point is behind left
edle point. Pass yarn under, then
er point of right needle.

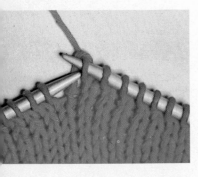

Draw yarn through stitch, forming
new stitch on the right needle. Let
tch on left needle slip off. Repeat
each stitch across the row.

Casting Off

1 Work first and second stitches of
the last row according to pattern
established in the directions.

2 Insert left needle into first stitch
from left to right. Lift stitch over
second stitch and off the right needle.

3 Slip stitch off left needle. One
stitch has been cast off. Repeat. To
end the work, cut the yarn and draw it
through the last stitch.

Tension Gauge

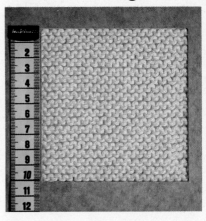

One key to successful knitting is working at the proper tension! Each
knitting direction is based on the
given tension gauge (number of rows
and stitches to 10 cm or 4″).

To check your tension, work a test
piece 12 cm or 5″ square in the stitch
pattern. Make a cardboard template
with a 10 cm or 4″ square cut out of it.
Place the template over your swatch
and count the rows and stitches. Compare the numbers with the tension
gauge given in the directions. If your
swatch has too few stitches and rows,
either knit more tightly or use smaller
needles. If you have more than the
number given, use larger needles.
Directions for the items shown can be
used for any yarn of similar thickness
and texture, providing you can achieve
the proper tension.

Decreasing, Increasing

Decreasing 1 stitch
Knit two stitches together.
Increasing 1 stitch
Knit stitch in usual way, but don't slip
it off the left needle. Knit again in the
back of the same stitch. Now slip the
stitch off the left needle.

1 Neutral shades are practical.　**2** Try a scarf of many colors.　**3** Make one in novelty yarns.　**4** Use a tweed yarn for texture.

Four scarves to knit

The longer, the better

Long, fringed scarves are not only warm, they are fashion news, too! And even beginners will find these scarves easy to knit because there is no purling.

Scarf 1
Materials Required:

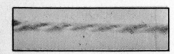

150 gm or 6 oz each of grey/green, white/green, and white/rust [50 gm = 155 m or 170 yds]. Knitting needles size 8 (Am) or 6 (Eng). Crochet hook.
Basic Stitch: Garter Stitch (knit every row), using 3 strands of yarn.
Tension: 15 stitches and 25 rows = 10 cm or 4".

Making the scarf
Cast on 24 stitches, using 3 strands of yarn (1 strand of each color). Knit scarf for 150 cm or 60".
Making the fringe
Cut 90 strands of each color 30 cm or 12" long. Knot 5 strands of each color into every 3rd stitch along the ends (see diagram on opposite page).

Scarf 2
Materials Required:

50 gm or 2 oz each of gold, yellow, pale green, dark green, grey, light blue, medium blue, dark blue, pink, rose, lilac. Knitting needles size 5 (Am) or 8 (Eng). Crochet hook.
Basic Stitch: Garter Stitch (knit every row).
Color Sequence: *Knit 3 rows each of yellow, pale green, dark green, grey, light blue, medium blue, dark blue, pink, rose, lilac, gold, repeat from *.
Tension: 22 stitches and 37 rows = 10 cm or 4".

Making the scarf
Cast on 33 stitches in gold. Knit 2 rows gold. Work Color Sequence 14 times, omitting gold rows in final sequence.
Making the fringe
Cut 12 strands 30 cm or 12" long of each color except medium blue. Knot 5 strands into every 3rd stitch along ends (see diagram). For cast-on row, use 1 strand each of pale green, dark green, yellow, gold, light blue. For cast-off row, use 1 strand pink, rose, lilac, dark blue, grey.

Scarves 3 & 4
Materials Required:

100 gm or 4 oz green or brown tweed. For fringe, 50 gm or 2 oz fine cotton, silk, or wool. Knitting needles size 5 (Am) or 8 (Eng). Crochet hook.
Basic Stitch: Garter Stitch (made by knitting every row).

Tension: 20 stitches and 34 rows = 10 cm or 4".

Making the scarf

Cast on 30 stitches. Knit until scarf measures 150 cm or 60".

Making the fringe

Cut 128 strands 40 cm or 16" long. Knot 4 strands into every other stitch along edge (see diagram). For silk fringe, make loop as shown in diagram, drawing strands through, then draw all strands through loop a second time. Pull tight.

JOINING STRANDS

When starting a new ball of yarn or changing colors, always join the new strand at the beginning of a row. Leave 10 cm or 4" of the old strand so that it can be woven into the piece. Leave 10 cm or 4" of the new strand at the edge and then work across the row. When the piece is finished, weave all ends neatly into the wrong side of the piece with a large-eyed tapestry needle.

MAKING FRINGE

Fold fringe strands in half. Insert crochet hook into edge from back to front and draw fringe loop through to back. Draw fringe ends through the loop and pull the knot tight.

Striped V-neck pullover
For the man in your life

urprise him with a
omfortable knitted
ull-on. The pattern is
arter stitch (every
w is knitted) and
u knit from side to
de to make long,
en vertical stripes.
e large V-neck
akes it easy to pull
and leaves plenty of
om for his favorite
irts to be seen. Knit
in colors which suit
s taste and style.

zes: Directions are for
cm (38") chest. Changes
100, 104 cm (39½",
") chest are in brackets.

aterials Required:

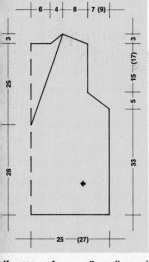

0 (300) gm or 9 (11) oz
ige, 150 gm or 6 oz dark
en, 50 gm or 2 oz orange.
0 gm = 140 m or 153
s]. Knitting needles
e 2 (Am) or 11 (Eng).

lf-pattern for smallest (largest)
es. Measurements are centimeters;
hes are given in the directions.

Basic Stitch: Garter stitch (knit every row).
Color Sequence 1: Knit 2 rows green, 8 rows beige.
Color Sequence 2: Knit 2 rows beige, 4 rows orange, 2 rows beige, 4 rows green.
Tension: 22 stitches and 50 rows = 10 cm or 4".

DIRECTIONS

Back: Cast on 73 stitches in beige. Work 7 rows beige, then continue in Color Sequence 1. *At the same time*, work left edge straight and shape armhole at right edge. Increase 11 stitches at regular intervals over the next 35 (40:45) rows – 84 stitches. Next row, cast on 33 (35:37) stitches at armhole – 117 (119:121) stitches.

Shape Shoulder: Knit 4 rows, then increase 1 stitch every 5th row 7 times – 124 (126:128) stitches.

Shape Neck: At overall length of 15 (16:17) cm or 6" (6¼":6½") decrease 1 stitch every 3rd row 7 times – 117 (119:121) stitches. Knit straight to 25 (26:27) cm or 10" (10¼":10½") for center back. Keeping to Color Sequence 1, knit other half of Back in reverse, being careful to increase where you decreased and decrease where you increased.

Front: Knit as for Back up to Shape Neck. At 15 (16: 17) cm or 6" (6¼":6½"), begin V-neck decrease. Alternately cast off 2 and 3 stitches every other row 25 times – 62 (64:66) stitches. Keeping to Color Sequence 1, knit other half of Front in reverse, being careful to increase where you decreased and decrease where you increased.

Hip Border: Cast on 110

(115:120) stitches in green. Knit 3 rows green, then Color Sequence 2 twice. Cast off the stitches.

Neck Border: Cast on 150 stitches in green. Knit 3 rows green, then Color Sequence 2 once, decreasing 1 stitch at each side of each row. Cast off the stitches.

Armhole Border: For each cast on 98 (102:106) stitches and knit 5 rows in green. Cast off.

Finishing: Sew front and back together, being careful to match colors at shoulders. Join each border at ends and stitch to bottom edge, neck, and armholes.

The pullover is knitted from side to side and a separate border piece is sewn on.

More suggestions: Perhaps he would prefer a solid-colored pullover with striped trim or a multi-colored one in another color combination.

Textured classic

Size: Directions are for 92 cm (36") bust. Changes for 96 cm and 100 cm (37½" and 39½") bust are in brackets.

Materials Required:

400 (450) gm or 15 (16) oz of each yarn [50 gm bouclé = 50 m or 54 yds; 50 gm plain = 70 m or 76 yds]. Knitting needles sizes 8 and 10 (Am); 6 and 3 (Eng).

Stitch Pattern 1: *Rows 1–4: With plain yarn and larger needles, knit odd-numbered rows and purl even-numbered rows. Rows 5–12: Change to bouclé yarn: purl the odd rows and knit the even rows. Repeat the pattern from *.

Stitch Pattern 2: With plain yarn and smaller needles, knit the odd rows and purl the even rows.

Border Pattern: Garter Stitch (knit every row).

Pattern 1 Tension: 13 sts and 22 R = 10 cm or 4".

Pattern 2 Tension: 15 sts and 22 R = 10 cm or 4".

Abbreviations: St(s) = stitch(es). R = row(s).

DIRECTIONS

Back: Cast on 65 (68: 70) sts with bouclé yarn and larger needles. Work Border Pattern for 9 R.
Work Stitch Pattern 1, decreasing 1 st at each side of every 10th R 4 times — 57 (60:62) sts. When piece measures 25 cm or 10", increase 1 st at each end of next R. Increase 1 st at each end of every 14th R 2 times — 63 (66:68) sts. Work

Simply classic

...ze: Directions are for
...4 cm (33") bust. Changes
...r 88, 92 cm (34½", 36")
...sts are in brackets.

...aterials Required:

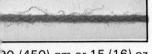

...00 (450) gm or 15 (16) oz
...ain color, 50 gm or 2 oz
...m color [100 gm = 300 m
... 328 yds]. Knitting
...eedles size 4 (Am) or 10
...ng). Two stitch holders.

...titch Pattern: Stocking
...Stockinette Stitch. **Note:**
...url side is the right side.

...ib Pattern: *Knit 2 sts,
...url 2 sts, repeat from *.

...ension: 24 sts and 35 R
... 10 cm or 4".

...bbreviations: St(s) =
...itch(es). R = row(s).

...IRECTIONS

...ack: Cast on 96 (102:
...06) sts in main color.
...Work 15 cm or 6" in Rib
...attern. Continue in Stitch
...attern and main color,
...creasing 1 st each side
...very 8 (8:7) rows 5 times —
...06 (112:116) sts. At 28
...5.5:27) cm or 11" (10¾":
...0½") cast on 2 (1:2) sts
...n each side — 110 (114:
...20) sts. End with a knit
...w. Place on stitch holder.

...ight Sleeve: Cast on 3
...ts in main color; work
...titch Pattern. At the right
...dge, increase 1 st every
...ther row 17 times for wrist
...dge. *At the same time*, at
...he left edge (inside sleeve
...eam), increase 2 and 3 sts
...lternately every other row
...7 times — 62 sts.
...When piece measures
...0 cm or 4", decrease 1 st
...t the right edge, then cast
...ff 2 sts every other row 13
...12:12) times. *At the same
...ime*, at the left edge,

...continued on page 22)

straight until piece measures 45 cm or 17¾".

<u>Shape Armholes:</u> At the beginning of every row, cast off 3 (3:4) sts 2 times, 2 sts 2 times, 1 st 2 times. Decrease 1 st at each end of every 4th R 2 times — 47 (50:50) sts. Work straight until piece measures 64 (65:66) cm or 25¼" (25⅝":26").

<u>Shape Shoulders:</u> At the beginning of every row, cast off 3 sts 3 times and 3 (4:4) sts 1 time.

At the same time, when the back measures 65 (66:67) cm or 25⅝" (26":26¾"), cast off middle 17 (18:18) sts for neck edge. At each side of neck edge, cast off 2 sts 1 time and 1 st 1 time.

<u>**Left Front:**</u> Cast on 38 (39:40) sts with bouclé yarn and larger needles. Work Border for 9 R.

Following Stitch Pattern 1, work increases and decreases at side, armhole, and shoulder as for back. *At the same time,* at 35 cm or 13¾", decrease 1 st at front edge, then decrease 1 st every 3rd row 9 times and 1 st every 4th row 7 times.

<u>**Right Front:**</u> As Left Front, reversing shapings.

<u>**Sleeves:**</u> Cast on 33 (35: 36) sts with bouclé yarn and smaller needles. Work Border Pattern for 8 cm or 3¼". Work Stitch Pattern 2, increasing 1 st at each end of every 6th R 11 times — 51 (53:56) sts. Work straight until piece measures 46 cm or 18⅛".

<u>Shape Armhole:</u> At the beginning of every row cast off: 3 sts 4 times, 2 sts 6 (6:4) times, 1 st 10 (10: 12) times, 2 sts 2 (2:4) times, 3 sts 4 times. Cast off 5 (7:6) sts.

Plain and bouclé yarns create an interesting texture contrast.

<u>**Front Edging:**</u> Cast on 7 sts with plain wool and smaller needles. R 1: *Knit 1, purl 1, repeat from * across. Work in rib for 160 cm or 63". Cast off.

<u>**Belt:**</u> Knit as for Front Edging for 150 cm or 60"

<u>**Finishing:**</u> Sew seams. Sew on Front Edging.

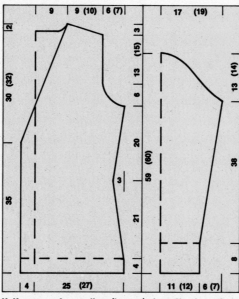
Half-patterns for smallest (largest) sizes. Numbers shown are centimeters; inches are given in directions.

Purling

Purl stitch produces the reverse effect of knit stitch. Purl stitch combined with knit stitch is the basis of most knitting, and alternating rows of knit and purl make the standard stocking or stockinette stitch. Many other textures and patterns can be created with various combinations of these stitches.

Increasing by casting on

This method does not require two strands of yarn and is ideal for adding stitches during knitting. However, it does not make as firm and hard-wearing an edge as the two-strand method and is not recommended for beginning most garments.

urling,
ncreasing by casting on

Hold yarn in front of the work.
nsert right needle into first stitch on
ft needle from right to left.

2 Left needle point is behind right needle point. Pass yarn over, then under point of right needle.

3 Draw yarn through stitch, forming a new stitch on right needle. Let stitch slip off left needle.

Make a slip knot on the left needle.
nsert the right needle into the loop
om left to right.

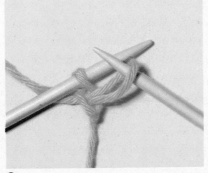

2 Pass yarn over, then under the point of the right needle and pull it through to form a new stitch.

3 Insert the left needle into the new stitch from right to left and slip it off the right needle.

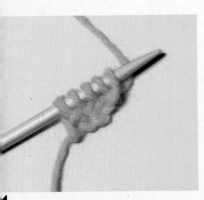

Do not pull the new stitch too
ight so that additional stitches may
e added. Hold yarn behind work.

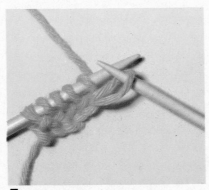

5 Insert right needle into the last stitch on the left needle from left to right, then repeat steps 2 and 3.

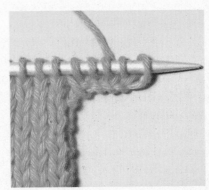

6 When increasing more than one stitch, cast on the required number at the end of a row.

increase 2 and 3 sts alternately every other row 14 (14:13) times — 70 (72: 69) sts. Work straight until piece measures 17 cm or $6\frac{3}{4}$". End with a knit row and place on stitch holder.

Left Sleeve: Work as for Right Sleeve, but work right edge increases and decreases at the left and left edge increases at the right. End with a knit row.

Shoulders: Purl across Right Sleeve, Back, then Left Sleeve—250 (258:258) sts. Decrease 2 sts at each end of every other row 34 (36:36) times — 114 sts. Work straight until piece measures 47 cm or $18\frac{1}{2}$", then in every other row at shoulder edge, cast off 3 sts 6 times and 7 sts 2 times. *At the same time,* at 48 cm or 19", cast off middle 30 sts for neck and work on each side separately. At neck edge, in every other row cast off 3 sts 2 times and 2 sts 2 times.

Front: Work as for Back (including sleeves) except for neck. At 40 cm or $15\frac{3}{4}$", cast off middle 10 sts. In every other row at neck edge, cast off 3 sts 3 times, 2 sts 3 times, and 1 st 2 times. Then cast off 1 st every 4th row 3 times.

Neck Border: Cast on 184 sts in trim color and work 3 cm or $1\frac{1}{4}$" in Rib Pattern. Cast off.

Cuffs: Cast on 64 sts in trim color and work 10 cm or 4" in Rib Pattern. Cast off. Repeat for other sleeve.

Finishing: Sew seams. Sew ends of border pieces together. Sew on neck border and cuffs, matching neck border seam to a shoulder seam and cuff seams to inside sleeve seam.

Each sleeve is worked in two halves which are knitted onto the front and back at the underarm.

Decreasing at the end of a row (See knitting how-to at right for decreasing at the beginning of a row):

Knitted decrease: Knit across to the last three stitches. Knit together the next two stitches. Knit the last stitch.

Purled decrease: Purl across to the last three stitches. Purl the next stitch and return it to the left needle. With the right needle, lift the middle stitch over the purled stitch. Return the purled stitch to the right needle. Purl the last stitch.

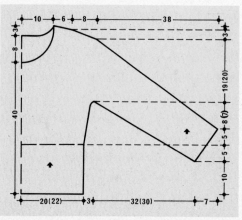

Half-pattern for smallest (largest) sizes. Numbers are centimeters; inches are given in directions.

Edge stitches

1 Chain Stitch Edge: Knit or purl the first stitch of every row according to the pattern stitch given in the direction. Work across the row.

Increasing

1 Knitted Increase: Knit the first stitch. Pick up the stitch below the next one and place it on the left needle. Knit this new stitch.

Decreasing

1 Knitted Decrease: Knit the first stitch. Insert right needle into second stitch and slip it onto right needle without working the stitch.

se the chain stitch edge for all finished outer edges of garments such as scarves and rdigans. The knot stitch edge can be used for seam edges.

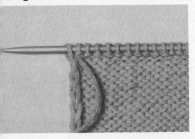

At the end of the row, insert right edle into the stitch as if to knit or rl, but transfer it onto the right edle without working it.

1 **Knot Stitch Edge:** Knit or purl the first stitch of every row according to the pattern stitch given in the directions. Work across the row.

2 At the end of every row, knit or purl last stitch according to the pattern. This creates a knotted edge on the wrong side of the piece.

ight edge increasing is shown here. Increase at the left edge by working across to last stitch left edge and picking up the new stitch from below the last stitch.

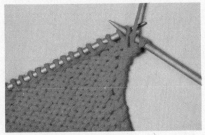

A new stitch has now been added knitting into a stitch from the evious row. Work the remaining tches on the left needle.

1 **Purled Increase:** Purl the first stitch. Pick up the stitch below the next one and place it on the left needle. Purl this new stitch in usual manner.

2 A new stitch has now been added by purling into a stitch from the previous row. Work the remaining stitches on the left needle.

 decorative edge can be made by decreasing so that the stitch slants inward. Decreasing the beginning of a row is shown below; decreasing at the end of a row is given at left.

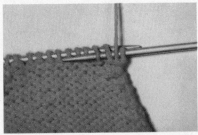

2 Knit the third stitch from the edge. nsert the left needle into the front of he slipped stitch on the right needle rom left to right.

3 Lift the slipped stitch over the last knitted stitch and off the right needle. Withdraw the left needle from the slipped stitch. Stitch slants to left.

1 **Purled Decrease:** Purl the first stitch. Insert the right needle into the next two stitches on the left needle and purl both the stitches together.

Bright sporting stripes

Children like bright stripes and they will be terribly proud of these sporty pullovers. You will appreciate the extra warmth they give when worn over a shirt or a jersey. They are made of stocking or stockinette stitch worked from side to side, and the ribbed borders are made separately and sewn on.

Size: Directions are for 74 cm (27″) chest. Changes for 68 cm (26″) chest are given in brackets.

Materials Required:

150 gm or 6 oz for background color. 50 gm or 2 oz for stripes and edging. (50 gm = 140 m or 153 yds). Knitting needles size 4 (Am) or 10 (Eng).

Stitch Pattern: Stocking or stockinette stitch (alternating knit and purl rows).

Rib Pattern: *Knit 1, purl 1, repeat from *.

Color Sequence: For white stripes on red: *2 R white, 6 R red, 2 R white, 2 R red, repeat from *. For red stripes on white: *2 R red, 6 R white, 2 R red, 2 R white, repeat from *.

Tension: 24 sts and 33 R = 10 cm or 4″.

Abbreviations: St(s) = stitch(es). R = row(s).

DIRECTIONS

Back: Cast on 48 (43) sts in background color. Work 3 (1) R Stitch Pattern in background color.

Shape Armhole: Begin Color Sequence. Keeping left (lower) edge straight, begin armhole shaping at right edge by increasing 1 st every other row 7 times, then 29 (26) sts 1 time — 84 (76) sts.

Shape Shoulder: Increase 1 st, then 1 st every 4th R 4 times (1 st every 3rd R 4 times) — 89 (81) sts.

Neck Edge: When piece measures 11.5 (10) cm or $4\frac{5}{8}″$ (4″) decrease every other row 2 sts 1 time and 1 st 3 times — 84 (76) sts. Work straight until piece measures about 18.5 (17) cm or $7\frac{1}{4}″$ ($6\frac{3}{4}″$) and you have reached the middle of a background-colored stripe. This is center back. Work other half to match, being careful to increase where you decreased and de-

crease where you increased. Cast off the stitches.

Front: Work for Back except for Neck edge. At 11.5 (10) cm or $4\frac{5}{8}$" (4") cast off 8 (5) sts in the 1st row and then in every 2nd row, cast off 3 sts 11 times — 48 (43) sts and center Front. Work other half to match. Cast off.

Lower Border: Cast on 84 (75) sts and work 6 cm or $2\frac{1}{2}$" in Rib Pattern. Cast off. Repeat for other piece.

Armhole Border: Cast on 92 (81) sts and work 2.5 cm or 1" in Rib Pattern. Cast off. Repeat for other Armhole Border.

Neck Border: Cast on 121 (111) sts and work 2.5 cm or 1" in Rib Pattern, increasing 1 st at each end of every row.

Finishing: Sew Lower Borders to Front and Back along cast-off rows of borders. Sew shoulder and side seams. Join ends of each Neck Border and sew in place along cast-off row.

The pullover is knitted from side to side. All of the border pieces are knitted separately and sewn on.

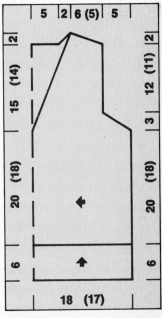

Half-pattern for larger (smaller) sizes. Measurements are centimeters; inches are given in the directions.

25

Relax luxuriously among
soft scatter pillows made in easy
knit-and-purl patterns.
Follow the charts at right for the
four designs shown here.

Quick and easy nitted geometrics

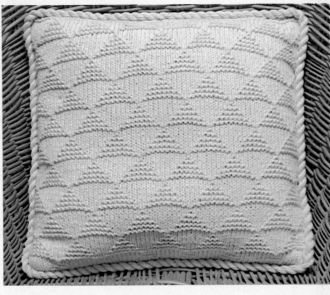

ize: 40 cm or 15¾″ quare.

Materials (for each):

50 gm or 13 oz [50 gm = 0 m or 87 yds]. Knitting eedles size 5 (Am) or 8 Eng). Thick white cording,

1.7 m or 1⅞ yds. Matching thread. Foam pillow or pieces for stuffing.

Tension: 18 sts and 30 R = 10 cm or 4″.

DIRECTIONS

Cast on 72 sts and work desired pattern for 232 R. Pattern charts are given below. Each symbol repre-

sents a stitch and solid lines indicate the end of the pattern repeat. When you have knitted to the line, go back to the beginning of the chart and begin the pattern again. Cast off stitches loosely.

Finishing: Fold in half, right sides together, and sew together along 2 sides

with backstitch. Turn to right side. Insert pillow and sew opening closed with slip stitch worked in each knitted stitch, leaving 2.5 cm or 1″ open for cord ends. Sew cording around edge with slip stitch. Overlap ends so cord looks continuous. Push ends into opening; slip-stitched closed.

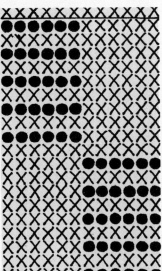

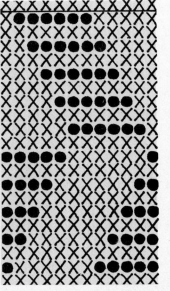

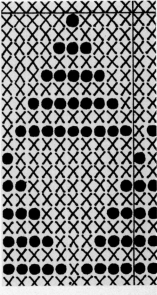

titch charts: Each symbol represents 1 stitch. Dots = purl stitches and Xs = knit stitches. The solid lines indicate the end of a pattern repeat.

Pullover in two versions

Knitted in the round

Size: Directions are for 88 cm (34½") bust. Changes for 92, 96 cm (36", 37½") bust are in brackets.

Materials Required:

(100 gm = 330 m or 380 yds.) See individual directions for yarn amounts. Circular needle and 5 double-pointed needles size 2 (Am) or 11 (Eng). Stitch Markers. Stitch holder.

Tension: 24 sts and 34 rnds = 10 cm or 4".

Abbreviations: •St(s) = stitch(es). R = row(s). Rnd(s) = round(s). K = knit. P = purl.

RIBBED PULLOVER

Yarn Required: 400 450:500) gm or 15 (16: 18) oz light brown.

Stitch Pattern: *K5, P5, repeat from *.

DIRECTIONS

Back and Front: Cast on 232 (242:252) sts. *P1 and mark as seam stitch, P5, work Stitch Pattern for 110 (115: 120) sts, repeat from * 1 time.

At 5 cm (2"), decrease 1

28

on each side of seam then in every 10th rnd times — 212 (222:232) s. Work straight until ece measures 22 cm or ¼". Increase 1 st on each de of seam st, then in ery 14th rnd 4 times — 32 (242:252) sts. At cm or 16½", cast off am sts and 7 sts on each de of them for underarms.

eeves: Using double-inted needles, cast on 2 sts and work in the und. K1 and mark as am st, K3, *P5, K5, peat from * 3 times, P5, 3 (K1 and mark for seam *P5, K5, repeat from * times, P1 : P1 and mark r seam st, P3, *K5, P5, peat from * 3 times, K5, 3). Continue Stitch Pattern d increase 1 st on each de of seam st every 9 rnds 7 times (every 8th rnd 19 nes : every 7th rnd 22 nes) — 86 (90:96) sts. t 47 cm or 18½", cast off am sts and 7 sts on each de of them for underarms. ace remaining sts on itch holder and knit other eeve in same way.

aglan Shaping: Add eeves to body on circular eedle (* on diagram = nnecting points) — 344 62:384) sts. In 1st rnd, it body edge st and sleeve ige st together at each de of the armholes — e decrease st and 2 sts either side of it form the aglan Band at each side of e armhole. Make sure sts ant toward center front d center back.

houlders: Decrease 1 st each side of the Raglan and in every other rnd 7 (29:32) times, then ecrease once on sleeve de only — 120 sts at 60 0.5:61) cm or 23½" 3¾":24"). Change to uble-pointed needles hen there are too few sts use the circular needle. eck: Work straight on 20 sts for 24 cm or 9½". ast off in pattern. inishing: Join seams.

Boat neck pullover is made from the same basic pattern as the ribbed version.

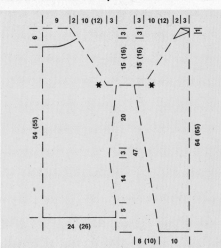

Half-pattern for both pullovers. The measurements are given in centimeters; inches are given in the directions.

STRIPED PULLOVER

Yarn Required: 200 (250: 250) gm or 7 (9:9) oz pale grey, 150 (200:200) gm or 6 (7:7) oz black.

Color Sequence: *2 rnds black, 2 rnds grey, repeat from *.

Border Pattern: *1 rnd purl, 1 rnd knit, repeat from * for required depth.

DIRECTIONS

Back and Front: Cast on 232 (242:252) sts in grey. Work Border Pattern for 3.5 cm or 1⅜", then continue in Color Sequence and knit every rnd. Mark 1st and 117th (122nd: 127th) sts as seam st. At 5 cm or 2", continue to work as for Ribbed Pullover to the end of each piece.

Sleeves: Using double-pointed needles, cast on 52 sts and work Border Pattern for 3.5 cm or 1⅜". Continue in Color Sequence and knit every rnd. *At the same time*, increase 1 st on each side of seam st every 9 rnds 17 times (every 8th rnd 19 times : every 7th rnd 22 times) — 86 (90:96) sts. At 47 cm or 18½", cast off seam sts and 7 sts on either side of them for underarms. Place remaining sts on stitch holder and knit other sleeve.

Raglan Shaping: Work as for Ribbed Pullover, making sure stripes match.

Shoulders: Decrease 1 st at each side of Raglan Band 23 (25:28) times on Front and 27 (29:32) times on back. *At the same time*, at 54 (54.5:55) cm or 21¼" (21⅜":21⅝"), cast off 26 sts at center front. Knit in open rows and at both ends of every other row, cast off 5 sts 2 times and 3 sts 8 times. Cast off remaining 46 sts.

Neck Border: Cast on 145 sts in grey and knit 3.5 cm or 1⅜" in Border Pattern. Cast off.

Finishing: Join underarm seams with overcasting. Sew on Neck Border.

Winter hats and scarves:

Striped, warm, and snug

You can ignore th[e]
winter chill with a
bright scarf wrapp[ed]
over your coat an[d]
matching hat pull[ed]
down over your e[ars.]

This scarf is knitted on the diagonal.

BOTH SETS
Stitch Pattern: Row 1: *Knit 1, purl 1, repeat from *. All other rows: knit the knit stitches and purl the purl stitches.

Materials Required:

[50 gm = 140 m or 150 yds]. Colors and amounts are given in individual directions. Knitting needles size 5 (Am) or 8 (Eng).

Tension: (unstretched): 28 sts and 28 R = 10 cm or 4".

Abbreviations: St(s) = stitch(es). R = row(s).

CANDY-STRIPES
Yarn Required: Scarf: 200 gm or 7 oz white, 50 gm or 2 oz red. Hat: 75 gm or 3 oz white, small amount red.

Scarf Color Sequence: *20 R white, 4 R red, repeat from *.

Making the scarf
Cast on 3 sts in white. Work in Color Sequence and Stitch Pattern with chain edge. At the right edge, increase 3 sts every other row 12 times. *At the same time*, at the left edge, increase 1 st every other row 12 times – 51 sts. The full width of the scarf has now been reached.
At the right edge, decrease 1 st every other row. At the left edge, continue to increase 1 st every 2nd R.
At 150 cm (60") from the cast-on edge, at the left edge, cast off 3 sts every other row 12 times, then 2 sts 1 time. *At the same time*, continue to decrease at the right edge.
Fringe: Cut yarn into 25 cm (10") pieces. Knot 2 strands into evenly spaced stitches across short ends.

Making the hat
Cast on 121 sts in white. Work straight in Stitch Pattern. At 3 cm ($1\frac{1}{4}$") knit 4 R red, finish in white.
At 25 cm (10") begin decreasing every other row.
Decrease 1: Knit together every 3rd and 4th sts (1 knit, 1 purl) by knitting into the backs of the sts – 91 sts. Decrease 2: Knit together every knit stitch which is followed by a purl stitch, by knitting into the backs of the sts – 61 sts. Decrease 3: Knit together every 5th and 6th sts as before – 51 sts. Continue to decrease thus in every 2nd R, working 1 st less between decreases each time until 11 sts remain. Draw a piece of yarn through the sts and fasten securely. Sew seam. Turn up lower 9 cm ($3\frac{1}{2}$").

MULTI-COLOR
Yarn Required: Scarf: 50 gm each of red, orange, gold, yellow, pale green, green. Hat: 75 gm or 3 oz red and small amounts of the other colors.

Making the scarf
Cast on 43 sts in red. Work straight in Stitch Pattern with chain edge. Work 25 cm (10") of each of the colors. Cast off.
Fringe: Cut yarn into 25 cm (10") pieces in the same colors as used at each end. Knot 2 strands into every knit st.

Making the hat
Cast on 121 sts in red. Work 56 R red, 6 R each of orange, gold, yellow, and pale green. Finish the hat in green.
At 25 cm (10"), work decreases and finishing as for candy-striped hat.

Knitting and crochet hints

Picking up a dropped knit stitch

If you drop a stitch in stocking or stockinette stitch, you can pick it up again without unraveling all of the knitting down to the row where the stitch was dropped. Pick up the dropped stitch from the knit side of the work with a crochet hook. Insert the hook into the loop of the dropped stitch with the hook facing upward. Hook the horizontal thread of the row above and pull it through the loop on the hook. Repeat for every row to the row presently on needles. Place the stitch on the left needle and continue to work across the row.

Unraveling knitting

Remove the needles from the piece; unravel to the row containing the mistake. Unravel this row stitch by stitch. Pick up the stitches with a finer needle than the one used to work the piece. Place the stitches on the needles, making sure that each stitch is turned in the right direction for the pattern. With the correct needle size, continue to work the piece.

Crochet turning chains

Chain stitches are needed at the end of each row to put the work in position for the next row. The chart below gives the number of chains required to turn.

Single crochet	chain 1
Half double crochet	chain 2
Double crochet	chain 3
Treble crochet	chain 4
Double treble	chain 5

Stitch markers

When the directions indicate that you are to mark a stitch, put a commercial ring marker, safety pin, or paper clip onto the needle or tie a piece of yarn in a contrasting color around the needle. When working across a row or a round, always transfer the marker from one needle to the other as you work past it.

Measuring a piece

Place the work on a flat surface and measure the length down through the center of the piece.

Running in ends

When you have finished the pieces, weave the yarn ends neatly into the work on the wrong side, by working them into the back of the stitches with a large-eyed tapestry needle. Weave in the ends for several inches so that they cannot work themselves out with subsequent wear and laundering. Trim ends close to work.

Blocking and pressing

To make professional-looking knitted or crocheted fashions, the way you assemble a garment is just as important as how well you knit or crochet it. When you have finished all of the pieces, there is always a great temptation to sew them together immediately so that you can see how stunning your creation is! However, if you will take the time to block the pieces to the proper size and shape before sewing the seams, you will find it much easier to assemble the garment, and the final results will be well worth the extra effort.

Blocking: Place the pieces, wrong side up, on a padded surface. Using rustproof pins and measuring to ensure the correct size, pin the pieces along all edges. Do not block the ribbings, but place pins across piece where the ribbing meets the flat stitches, to hold the flat stitches in place.

Damp cloth method: Cover the pieces with a damp cloth and leave them until the pieces and the cloth are completely dry.

Dry iron pressing (for flat textures): Cover the pieces with a damp cloth and hold a dry iron over the cloth so that the steam penetrates the yarn. Do not press down or slide the iron over the surface. Do not hold the iron in one place too long.

Steam iron pressing (for novelty yarns and pattern stitches): This method does not require a damp cloth. Hold the steam iron close to the piece, but do not let it touch the yarn. Move the iron slowly, letting the steam penetrate the yarn. When the pieces are completely dry, remove the pins and assemble the garment. Press the seams with the dry or steam iron method.

Joining seams

Sew seams with a blunt-ended needle and the yarn used to make the garment. If the yarn is too thick, for easy stitching, split the yarn or use thinner yarn in the same color. Pin the pieces, right sides together, and sew the seam with back-stitch or embroidered chain stitch a half stitch or one stitch away from the edge. Be careful to work in a straight line and not to split the stitches. Do not pull the stitches too tight or make them too loose.

Laundering hints

To maintain the proper shape of the garment, trace around it with a pencil on brown wrapping paper. Spread the paper out over several layers of newspaper or bath towels to protect the surface below it from the damp garment.

Wash wool yarns, including angora, in lukewarm water with soap or mild detergent. Synthetic yarns can be washed in warmer water. Squeeze the suds gently through the garment. To prevent stretching, do not twist or wring it or lift it out of the water without supporting it in your hands. Rinse thoroughly in water of the same temperature to remove all soap or detergent. You may use a softening agent in the final rinse if desired.

Place towels over and under the garment, then roll and squeeze gently to remove excess water.

Place the garment on the brown paper and put it gently into the pencilled outline. Allow it to dry completely. If washing angora, fluff up the hairs before it is completely dry; refluff when dry. Usually, garments will not need to be pressed after laundering. However, if it does need pressing, follow the pressing directions given with blocking and pressing.

Knitting in the round

You knit round and round, without turning the piece and working back across the row, to produce a seamless knitted tube.

Double-pointed needles and circular needle

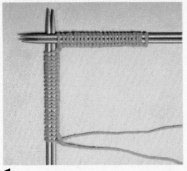

1 Cast half the required number of stitches onto two pairs of double-pointed needles.

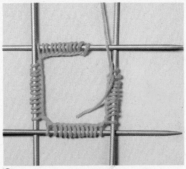

2 Remove a needle from each pair. Divide stitches among four needles; knit with fifth needle.

3 Use a circular needle for large tubular pieces. Be careful not to twist the cast-on round.

Decreasing and increasing for a simple heel

1 **Decreasing:** At end of row, leave one stitch unworked. Turn. In following rows, leave one more stitch unworked.

2 At beginning of each row, transfer one stitch to the right needle without working it. Keep unworked stitches on the needles.

3 **Increasing:** At the end of every row, work one more unworked stitch held on the left needle.

4 At the beginning of the row, slip an unworked stitch to left needle to add a stitch to the row.

Knitting two stitches together

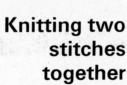

Insert right needle into the two stitches from left to right. Work knit stitch as usual.

These versatile fashions are easy to make

In Chain Stitch and Single Crochet

Here are some fashion tips for you: crochet the long-sleeve pullover to co-ordinate with your casual clothes or make the other top in metallic yarn for evening. Or make them both — they'll add endless variety to your wardrobe. The glittery sleeveless top also looks smart with shirts and the long-sleeve version is pretty with velvet pants at night. The open-work pattern is easier than it looks! It's made entirely of chain stitch and single crochet, and once you have learned the two basic stitches, you don't have to be an expert to make these exciting designs.

Size: Directions are for 88 cm (34½″) bust. Changes for 92 cm (36″) bust are in brackets.

Materials Required:

400 gm or 15 oz for long-sleeve style; 300 gm or 11 oz for sleeveless style [100 gm = 490 m or 535 yds]. Crochet hook size D.

Stitch Pattern: Rows 1–4: Work ribbed single crochet in 2nd stitch from hook and in each stitch across. Chain 1, turn the work.

Row 5: Chain 5, 1 single crochet into 4th stitch of previous row. *Chain 5, 1 single crochet into 3rd stitch from previous single crochet, repeat from * across. Chain 2, turn work.

Row 6: *3 single crochet into each chain-5 loop, repeat from * to last chain-5 loop; 4 single crochet into last loop. Chain 1, turn.

Tension: 26 stitches and 23 rows of single crochet = 10 cm or 4″.

DIRECTIONS

Back: Chain 68.

Right Armhole: Single crochet in 2nd chain from hook and in each chain across — 67 stitches. Chain 1, turn. Work Stitch Pattern for 8 (14) rows.

At the end of the 8th (14th) pattern row, chain 46. Single crochet in 2nd chain from hook and in each chain or single crochet across row —112 stitches. Chain 1, turn the work.

Right Shoulder: Continue to work Stitch Pattern for 21 more rows.

Neck: Work next row (3 single crochets in chain-5 loops), but omit single crochets in last 2 loops — 105 stitches. Chain 2, turn. Work pattern on 105 stitches for 40 more rows.

At the end of the 40th row, chain 7, turn. Chain 5, single crochet in 10th chain from hook, *chain 5,

Crochet

The texture of the pullover looks completely different, depending on the yarn used. A sparkling yarn has been used here to give it a party look.

Extra rows of single crochet are worked at each edge of the neck. Be careful not to distort the pattern when overlapping and sewing the corners in place.

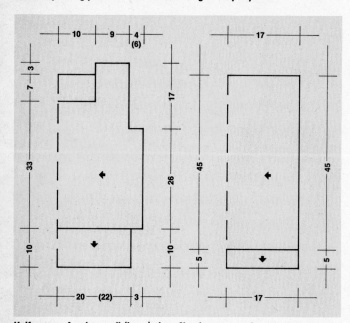

Half-pattern for the small (large) sizes. Numbers are centimeters; inches are in the directions. Arrows indicate direction to crochet each piece.

single crochet in 3rd stitch from previous single crochet, repeat from * across. Chain 2, turn.

Left Shoulder: Work 3 single crochets in each chain-5 loop across row; work 4 single crochets in last chain-5 loop — 112 stitches. Chain 1, turn. Work Stitch Pattern for 19 more rows.

Left Armhole: Work only 67 single crochets in the next row. Work pattern on 67 stitches for 8 (14) rows.

Front: Right Armhole and Shoulder: Work as for back.

Neck: Work next row (3 single crochets in chain-5 loops), but omit single crochets in last 8 loops — 87 stitches. Chain 2, turn. Work Stitch Pattern for 40 more rows.

At the end of the 40th row, chain 25, turn. Chain 5, single crochet in 10th chain from hook. *Chain 5, single crochet in 3rd stitch from previous single crochet, repeat from * across. Chain 2, turn the work.

Left Shoulder and Armhole: Work as for back.

Ribbing: Chain 105 (115). Single crochet into 2nd chain from hook and into each chain across — 104 (114) stitches. Chain 1, turn. Work in ribbed single crochet for 10 cm or 4". Repeat for front.

Sleeves (optional): Chain 119. Single crochet in 2nd chain from hook and in each chain across — 118 stitches. Chain 1, turn. Work Stitch Pattern for 34 cm or 13½". Repeat for other sleeve. For

cuffs, work 88 ribbed single crochets across one short end for 5 cm or 2".

Finishing: Both: Sew ribbed borders to front and back, gathering front and back slightly to border width. Join front and back at shoulder seams. Work 5 ribbed rows of 34 single crochets at each side of neck. Work 5 ribbed rows of 54 single crochets at front and back of neck. Sew ends of front and back edgings over side edgings as illustrated above. Sew side seams.

Sleeveless Pullover: At lower edge of each armhole, work 5 ribbed rows of 22 (32) single crochets. Overlap and sew as for neck.

Long Sleeve Pullover: Work 2 ribbed rows of 88 single crochets at top edge of sleeve. Sew top edge of sleeve to armhole, sewing 4 cm or 1⅝" at bottom of underarm to 4 cm or 1⅝" at each side of sleeve seam. Sew remainder of seam.

Chain stitch, Single crochet

Crochet always begins with chain stitch. Be careful to make all the stitches the same size so your work has a neat edge. To end the piece, cut the yarn and draw it through the last loop on the hook.

Chain Stitch

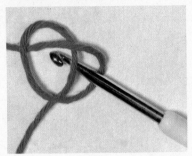

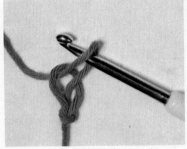

1 Arrange yarn as shown. With a crochet hook, draw the bottom strand through to form a loop. Pull the knot close to the hook.

2 Hold work between index finger and thumb to control the tension. Pass the hook under strand from ball of yarn and catch it with hook.

3 Draw strand through loop to form the first chain stitch. Repeat steps 2 and 3 until you have made the required number of stitches.

Single Crochet

1 Insert hook from front to back into second chain from hook. Pass yarn over hook; draw it through chain, making two loops on hook.

2 Pass yarn over hook and draw it through both loops already on the hook to form a single crochet. There is one loop left on the hook.

3 Repeat steps 1 and 2 across the row. At the end of the row, chain 1 stitch and turn the work to bring it into position for the next row.

4 For all other rows, begin with second stitch and repeat steps 1 and 2 across row. Work under both strands of stitches in previous row.

5 To create a **ribbed pattern in single crochet**, insert hook only under back strand of each stitch, then work the stitch in usual way.

Tension Gauge

Each crochet direction is based on the given tension gauge. To check your tension, crochet a test piece 12 cm or 5″ square in the pattern stitch. Make a cardboard template with a 10 cm or 4″ square cut out of it. Place the template over your swatch and count the rows and stitches. If you have more than the number given in the directions, crochet more loosely or use a larger hook. If you have too few rows and stitches, crochet more tightly or use a smaller hook.

An unbeatable top team

A matching hat and vest — an eyecatching team for topping a wardrobe of plain and patterned shirts and pullovers. The look is young and sporty, and the easy double crochet pattern makes quick work of it all!

Size: Vest: Directions are for 84 cm (33″) bust. Changes for 88 cm and 92 cm (34½″ and 36″) busts are in brackets. Hat: 54 cm (21¼″).
Abbreviations: St(s) = stitch(es). R = row(s).

STRIPED SET
Materials Required:

Work the hat and matching vest in yellow as a bright accent for a plaid shirt.

100 gm or 4 oz brown. 50 gm or 2 oz each beige, green, red, rust, blue, yellow [100 gm = 360 m or 390 yds]. Crochet hook size E.
Basic Stitch: Double crochet. (At the end of each row, chain 3 to turn).
Color Sequence: *6 R brown, 2 R beige, 2 R green, 2 R red, 6 R brown, 2 R rust, 2 R blue, 2 R yellow, repeat from *.
Tension: 19 sts and 12 R = 10 cm or 4″.

Making the vest
Back: Chain 87 (91:95) sts in brown. Work double crochet in 4th chain from hook and in each chain across — 84 (88:92) sts. Work straight in Basic Stitch and Color Sequence for about 32 cm or 12½″.

Shape Armholes: At the end of the next 2 R, leave 13 (14:15) sts unworked — 58 (60:62) sts. Work straight until piece measures 48 cm or 19″.
Shape Neck and Shoulders: Leave middle 26 sts unworked. Work shoulders for 2 R on 16 (17:18) sts at each end.
Left Front: Chain 32 (34: 36) sts in brown. Work double crochet in 4th chain from hook and in each

chain across — 29 (31: 33) sts. Work straight in Basic Stitch and Color Sequence until the piece measures 32 cm or 12½″.
Shape Armholes: Leave 13 (14:15) sts at right edge unworked. Work straight on 16 (17:18) sts until piece measures 50 cm or 19½″.
Right Front: Work as for left front, but make armhole at left edge.
Finishing: Sew seams at sides and shoulders. Work

39

The directions are given for two different types of yarn. The finer yarn creates a multi-season vest to wear with lightweight shirts. The heavier yarn produces larger stitches and a bolder look which teams well with coarse shirt fabrics and pullovers.

Crochet

1 R double crochet with main color along front, neck, armhole edges.

Making the hat
Chain 107 sts in brown. Work double crochet in 4th chain from hook and in each chain across — 104 sts. Work straight in Basic Stitch, working 5 R brown, 1 R each beige, green, red, brown, rust, blue, yellow, 10 R brown.
Sew side edges together. For center top, make running stitch through last row of double crochet. Draw stitches together tightly and secure in place.

YELLOW SET
Materials Required:

350 gm or 13 oz yellow [50 gm = 85 m or 92 yds]. Crochet hook size H.
Basic Stitch: Double crochet. (At the end of each row, chain 3 for turning.)
Tension: 16 sts and 8½ R = 10 cm or 4".

Making the vest
Back: Chain 73 (75:79) sts in yellow. Work double crochet in 4th chain from hook and in each chain across — 70 (72:76) sts. Work straight in Basic Stitch for 32 cm or 12½".
Shape Armholes: Leave 11 (12:13) sts at each end of the next row unworked. Work straight on 48 (48:50) sts. Work straight until piece is 48 cm or 19".
Shape Neck: Leave middle 22 sts unworked. Work shoulders for 2 R on 13 (13:14) sts at each end.

Left Front: Chain 27 (28:30) sts in yellow. Work double crochet in 4th chain from hook and in each chain across — 24 (25:27) sts. Work straight in Basic Stitch for 32 cm or 12½".
Shape Armhole: Leave 11 (12:13) sts at right edge unworked. Work straight on 13 (13:14) sts until piece measures 50 cm or 19½".
Right Front: Work as for left front, but make armhole at left edge.
Finishing: Finish as for Striped Set.

Making the hat
Chain 89 sts in yellow. Work double crochet in 4th chain from hook and in each chain across — 86 sts. Work straight in Basic Stitch for 20 cm or 8".
Sew side edges together. For center top, make running stitch through last row of double crochet. Draw stitches together.

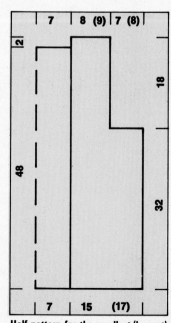

Half-pattern for the smallest (largest) sizes. Numbers are centimeters; inches are given in directions.

Double crochet

Double crochet is similar to single crochet, but makes deeper, more open rows.

1 To begin double crochet, pass the hook under, then over the yarn as illustrated above.

2 Insert hook under both strands of stitch in previous row. Pass the hook under, then over the yarn.

3 Draw yarn through stitch to make three loops on the hook. Pass hook under, then over the yarn.

4 Draw the yarn through the first two loops on the hook. There are now two loops on the hook.

5 Pass the hook under, then over the yarn and draw it through the two stitches on the hook.

6 One double crochet has been completed and one loop remains on hook. Repeat steps 1–5 across row.

Crazy crocheted patchwork

Create a one-of-a-kind afghan — the final result depends on the colors you choose and the patterns you make! Even the same design worked in other colors gives a totally different effect.

Crochet

We have chosen three of the squares and give the directions below. You can design many variations which can be adapted from these patterns. The color choice is up to you, and the more colors you use, the more interesting your afghan will be.

For all squares

Size: Each square = 17 cm (6¾"). Our afghan is made from 104 squares arranged in 13 rows of 8 squares. It measures about 135 × 220 cm (54" × 88").

Materials Required:

We used white, black, pale blue, blue, and turquoise. However, there is no limit to the number of colors you can use. Crochet hook F.

Making the squares

The directions for making up the squares are given at right. If desired, you can use the same color around the outside edge of each square to make a framed effect. When all of the squares are finished and you have planned their arrangement, crochet the squares together with slip stitch. Place 2 squares side

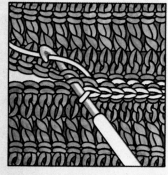

Join squares together with slip stitch.

by side with right sides down. Attach yarn at corner. Draw yarn through so there is a loop on the hook. Insert hook into each corner stitch and draw yarn through stitches and loop on hook. Continue in this way across the row. Attach squares in long strips, then crochet strips together.

Corner square

Chain 6 in turquoise.

Row 1: Beginning in 4th stitch from hook, work 3 double crochets, chain 3, turn the work.

Row 2: Work 1 double crochet into each double crochet of the previous row, work 4 double crochets around the turning chain loop, chain 3, turn.

Row 3: This and all following rows begin in the 1st double crochet and end with a chain-3 for turning. Double crochet into each of the next 3 stitches, 3 double crochet into the next stitch, double crochet into each of the next 4 stitches.

Row 4: Double crochet into every double crochet of the previous row, working 3 double crochets into the middle stitch at the corner.

Rows 5–13: Repeat row 4 in the following color sequence: 2 rows white, 3 rows blue, 2 rows turquoise, 2 rows black.

Row 14 (white): Work double crochet into each stitch to corner stitch; 2 double crochet, chain 2, 2 double crochet into corner stitch; work double crochet in each stitch to end of row; chain 1, turn.

Row 15 (white): Beginning in the 2nd stitch, work single crochet in each stitch to corner stitch; 5 single crochet in corner stitch; work single crochet in each stitch to end of row; chain 1, turn the work.

Row 16 (turquoise): Beginning in the 1st stitch, work 1 single crochet in each stitch to corner stitch; 3 single crochet in corner stitch; work single crochet in each stitch to end of row.

Note: 4 motifs can be joined to make 1 square.

Checkerboard

The 4 squares are crocheted gradually onto one another. Chain 15. Double crochet into 2nd chain from hook and in each chain across, chain 3, turn. Work 6 more double crochet rows. Each square is 7 rows deep and 12 double crochets plus a chain-3 wide.

Begin with the white square. Fasten black yarn onto the white chain row and work in the opposite direction. Fasten blue yarn into last double crochet of the white square and work square along side of white square. For the second white square, fasten yarn into black square where all squares meet. Chain 3, slip-stitch into adjacent blue double crochet, then 12 double crochet along black edge. Finish square, working slip stitch into the blue square to join the two. Slip-stitch around the edge.

Granny square

Chain 5, slip-stitch into 1st chain to form a ring. Work with right side facing.

1st Round (white): Chain 3, 3 double crochet around the ring. *Chain 2, 4 double crochet around the ring, repeat from * 2 times, chain 2. Close all rounds with a slip stitch.

2nd Round (blue): In a chain-2: chain 3, 3 double crochet, chain 2, 4 double crochet. In each following corner: 4 double crochet, chain 2, 4 double crochet.

3rd–6th Rounds (turquoise, black, white, pale blue): In a chain-2: chain 3, 3 double crochet, chain 2, 4 double crochet. In each space between groups of 4 double crochets: 4 double crochet. In each corner: 4 double crochet, chain 2, 4 double crochet.

7th Round (blue): In a chain-2: chain 3, 7 double crochet. In each space between groups of 4 double crochets: 4 double crochet. In each corner: 8 double crochet.

Note: You can make the squares more open by working 3 double crochets rather than 4.

You can also make squares any size — even a large one-square coverlet. Just continue working rounds and increasing at the corners.

Slip stitch, Shaping corners

When working pieces of square or rectangular crochet, you must be able to shape corners and close the rounds, otherwise your pieces will not lie flat or be the proper shape. The slip stitch can also be used to make neat edges and crochet the pieces together when they are finished.

Shaping corners

1 Without a hole: Work five double crochets into corner stitch. In all following rounds, work into middle double crochet at the corner.

Slip stitch

1 Every round is closed with a slip stitch. Insert hook into last stitch of the turning chain of the last round. Catch yarn with hook.

2 With a hole: 2 double crochet, chain 1, 2 double crochet into corner stitch. In the following rounds, work around the chain stitch.

2 Draw yarn through stitch and loop on hook to end the round. To make a neat edge, work slip stitch into all the stitches of last round.

3 Granny square: In first round, chain 2, at each corner. Thereafter: 3 double crochet, chain 2, 3 double crochet into the chain-2.

Crochet

Size: Directions are for 84 cm (33") bust. Changes for 88, 92 cm (34½", 36") bust are in brackets.

Materials Required:

100 gm or 4 oz purple (red), 50 gm or 2 oz white [40 gm = 230 m or 250 yds]. Crochet hook size D.

Stitch Pattern: *1 double crochet into double crochet in previous row, chain 1, skip chain and double crochet into next double crochet, repeat from *, chain 3, turn.

Color Sequence: *2 R purple (red), 2 R white, repeat from *.

Border Stitch: Single crochet.

Tension: 37 sts and 18 R = 10 cm or 4".

Abbreviations: St(s) = stitch(es). R = row(s). Dc = double crochet.

DIRECTIONS

Back: Chain 80 (79:78) sts in purple (red). Dc in 6th chain from hook, *chain 1, dc in 2nd chain from last dc, repeat from * across. Chain 3, turn. Chain 1, continue in Stitch Pattern and Color Sequence, working straight at bottom edge. *At the same time,* at right edge increase 1 st every R 12 times for armhole — 89 (88:87) sts. At 7 cm or 2¾", chain 63

(64:65) sts for shoulde Dc in 6th chain from hoc and work across row Stitch Pattern — 149 st Increase 1 st alternate every R and every 2nd (alternately every R an every 2nd R: every 2nd F 8 times — 157 sts. At 14 (15:16) cm or 5½ (6":6¼"), decrease 2 sts a neck every R 4 times — 14 sts. Work straight to 22 (2: 24) cm or 8½" (9":9½" center Back. Work the othe

Stripes for all seasons

half in reverse, being careful to increase where you decreased and decrease where you increased. Work Hip Border on bottom edge.

Front: Work as for Back until piece is 14 (15:16) cm or 5½″ (6″:6¼″). Work V-neck by decreasing 6 sts in every R 14 times at center front. Work other half in reverse. Work Hip Border along the bottom edge as for Back.

Hip Border: Single crochet along bottom edges in purple (red) on 86 (91:96) sts for 10 cm or 4″.

Neck Border: Chain 150 in purple (red). Work 6 R in Border Pattern, decreasing 1 st at each end of every R.

Armhole Border: For each, chain 100 (103:106) in purple (red). Work 6 R in Border Pattern, decreasing 1 st at each end of every R.

Finishing: Sew seams. Join ends of Border pieces and sew in place.

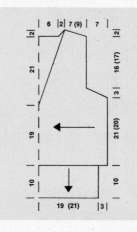

Multiple-stitch decrease
To decrease more than 1 stitch at the beginning of a row, slip-stitch required number of stitches. To decrease more than 1 stitch at the end of a row, leave the required number of stitches unworked.

◀ Half-pattern for smallest (largest) sizes. Measurements are centimeters; inches are given in directions. Crochet in the direction of the arrows.

Increasing, Decreasing

Increasing 1 stitch

1 Increasing 1 stitch at the beginning of a row: Begin in the first stitch of the previous row rather than the second stitch after the turning chain.

2 Increasing 1 stitch within the row or at the end of a row: Work two stitches into one stitch or turning chain of the previous row.

Decreasing 1 stitch

1 Decreasing 1 stitch: Insert hook and draw yarn through the next two stitches, keeping the loops on the hook and not completing the stitches.

2 Pass the yarn over the hook and draw it through all three stitches on the hook. The decrease can be worked within a row or at either edge.

Decreasing, Increasing (Filet crochet)

1 **Decreasing:** At the beginning of the row, chain across the stitches to be decreased. At the end of the row, skip the next to the last stitch.

2 **Increasing:** Work additional chain stitches at the beginning of the row. In the next row, work additional stitches into the chain.

Triangular
mesh shawl

Delicate and yet so warm

This airy mesh shawl has a romantic look, but it's practical and warm, too.

Materials Required:

400 gm or 15 oz black [50 gm = 70 m or 76 yds]. Crochet hook size K.

Tension: 11 sts and 5 R = 10 cm or 4".

Abbreviations: St(s) = stitch(es). R = row(s). Dc = double crochet.

DIRECTIONS

Begin the shawl at the lower point. The work is increased by one square in every row.

Row 1: Chain 12. Dc into 1st chain. Chain 11, turn.

Row 2: Dc into base of turning chain, chain 4, 1 dc into 4th chain from last dc, chain 11, turn.

Row 3: 1 dc into base of turning chain, chain 4, dc into next dc, chain 4, dc into 4th chain from last dc, chain 11, turn.

Row 4: 1 dc into base of turning chain, *chain 4, dc into next dc, repeat from * and work into every dc of previous row, chain 4, dc into 4th chain from last dc, chain 11, turn.

Repeat Row 4 until shawl measures 45 cm or 18".

Finishing: For fringe, cut 40 cm or 16" pieces of yarn and knot 6 into every square along the side edges.

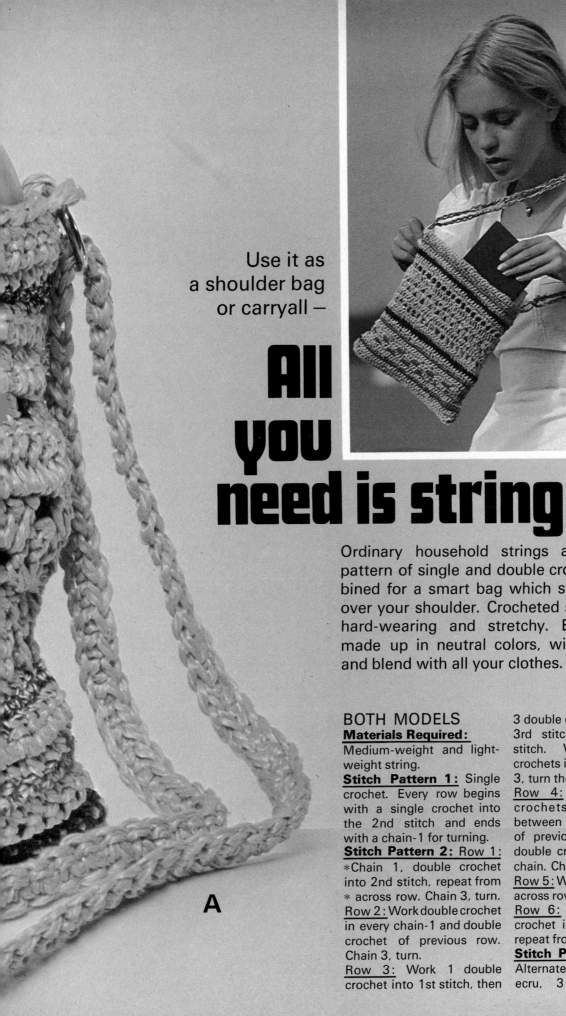

Use it as
a shoulder bag
or carryall —

All you need is string

Ordinary household strings and a crochet pattern of single and double crochet are combined for a smart bag which swings casually over your shoulder. Crocheted string makes it hard-wearing and stretchy. Either version, made up in neutral colors, will complement and blend with all your clothes.

BOTH MODELS

Materials Required:
Medium-weight and light-weight string.

Stitch Pattern 1: Single crochet. Every row begins with a single crochet into the 2nd stitch and ends with a chain-1 for turning.

Stitch Pattern 2: Row 1: *Chain 1, double crochet into 2nd stitch, repeat from * across row. Chain 3, turn.

Row 2: Work double crochet in every chain-1 and double crochet of previous row. Chain 3, turn.

Row 3: Work 1 double crochet into 1st stitch, then 3 double crochets into every 3rd stitch across to last stitch. Work 2 double crochets in last stitch. Chain 3, turn the work.

Row 4: Work 3 double crochets into spaces between 3 double crochets of previous row. Work 1 double crochet into turning chain. Chain 3, turn.

Row 5: Work double crochet across row. Chain 3, turn.

Row 6: *Chain 1, double crochet into second stitch, repeat from * across row.

Stitch Pattern 3: Row 1: Alternate 3 single crochets ecru, 3 single crochets

A

Crochet

green/white (see sketch on next page). The color not in use is carried behind the work and picked up from beneath the other strand.

Row 2: Repeat row 1, working into ecru stitches with ecru and into green/white with green/white.

Row 3: Work as for row 1, but reverse color sequence.

Row 4: Repeat row 3.

Abbreviations: St(s) = stitch(es). R = row(s).

Note: Use all lightweight string doubled.

MODEL A

Size: 26 cm (10¼") wide × 23 cm (9") high.

Materials Required: 3 balls of medium-weight string in ecru. 1 ball each of lightweight string in brown, blue/white, green/white, red/yellow. Crochet hook size H. 2 metal rings, about 3 cm (1¼") diameter.

Tension: 14 sts and 16 R = 10 cm or 4".

DIRECTIONS

Chain 74 with ecru string. Single crochet in 2nd chain

Secure the straps with metal rings.

from hook and in each chain across — 73 sts. Following Stitch Pattern 1, work 3 R ecru, 2 R brown, 2 R ecru, 1 R red/yellow, 2 R ecru, 2 R blue/white, 1 R ecru. With ecru string, work Stitch Pattern 2. Following Stitch Pattern 1, work 3 R ecru, 2 R green/white, 3 R ecru.

Strap: Chain 225 with ecru string. Single crochet in 2nd chain from hook and in each chain across.

Finishing: Sew side seam and bottom. Sew rings at each side. Pull strap through both rings and sew ends.

Common household strings are available in a wide variety of sizes and colors.

MODEL B

Size: 21 cm (8¼") square.

Materials Required: Lightweight string: 4 balls ecru, 1 ball each of brown, green/white and red/yellow. Crochet hooks sizes D and H. 2 metal rings, about 3 cm (1¼") diameter.

Tension: 19 sts and 21 R = 10 cm or 4".

DIRECTIONS

Chain 83 with ecru string and D hook. Single crochet in 2nd chain from hook and in each chain across — 82 sts. Working Stitch Pattern 1, crochet 3 R ecru, 2 R green/white, 2 R ecru. Work Stitch Pattern 3. Following Stitch Pattern 1, work 2 R ecru, 2 R green/white, 2 R brown, 2 R ecru.

Work Stitch Pattern 2 with ecru yarn. Working Stitch Pattern 1, crochet 2 R each of ecru, brown, ecru, red/yellow. In following row alternate 2 sts ecru, 2 sts red/yellow. Work 2 R ecru.

Strap: Chain 200 with H hook and 1 strand each of ecru, green/white, and red/yellow or desired colors.

Finishing: Assemble as for other bag.

Work three double crochets into the space between groups in the previous row.

Carry yarn behind work. Pick up new color from under old one to prevent a hole.

Fun – and practical, too

my favorite skirt has lots of stripes

Your little daughter will love this skirt because it is bright and colorful. You will love it because you can lengthen it by crocheting extra rows along the top as she grows. Try it, and see how pretty it looks with her favorite blouses or pullovers.

Size: Waist: 55, 53.5, 52 cm (21½", 21", 20½"). Corresponding lengths: 24, 22, 21 cm (9½", 8⅝", 8¼"). Directions for the two smaller sizes are given in brackets.

Materials Required:

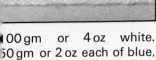

100 gm or 4 oz white. 50 gm or 2 oz each of blue, orange, red, and yellow. Crochet hook size D. Two buttons.

Color Sequence: *2 R each of blue, white, red, orange, yellow, white, repeat from *.

Stitch Pattern: Alternating chain-1 and single crochet stitches.

Decreasing 1 st (for chain-1, single crochet pattern): Pass yarn over hook, but do

It is so practical, because you can lengthen it by adding extra rows as she grows.

not pull it through stitch on hook. Insert hook into chain-1 and pull yarn through chain-1 (3 loops on hook). Pass yarn over hook and pull through all 3 loops.

Tension: 29 sts and 25 R of Stitch Pattern = 10 cm or 4".

Abbreviations: St(s) = stitch(es). R = row(s).

Note: Unless otherwise specified, single crochet is worked into chain-1 in previous row.

DIRECTIONS

Back: Chain 141 (133: 131) with blue yarn.

Row 1: Single crochet into 3rd chain from hook, *chain 1, single crochet in 2nd chain from previous single crochet, repeat from * across — 139 (131:129) sts. Chain 1, turn.

Row 2: Chain 1, *single crochet, chain 1, repeat from * across. After last chain-1, single crochet in turning chain of previous row with next color, chain 1, turn the work.

Row 3: Single crochet, *chain 1, single crochet, repeat from * across. Chain 1, turn the work.

Row 4: Repeat row 2.

Row 5: Repeat row 3. From this point on, decrease 1 st at the end of every row as follows:

Row 6: Chain 1, *single crochet, chain 1, repeat from * across, but do not make last chain-1. With next color, chain 1, turn.

Row 7: Chain 1, *single crochet, chain 1, repeat from * across to last 2 sts, decrease 1 st. Chain 1, turn.

Row 8: Single crochet into decrease in previous row, *chain 1, single crochet, repeat from * across to last 2 sts, decrease 1 st. With next color, chain 1; turn.

Row 9: Single crochet into decrease in previous row, *chain 1, single crochet, repeat from * across, but do not make last chain-1. Chain 1, turn.

Repeat rows 6–9 until 81 (79:77) sts remain.

Front: Work as for Back.

Straps: Chain 147 (143: 139) with white yarn. Crochet 6 R in Stitch Pattern, working 2 R each of white, blue, white.

For buttonhole: 4 cm or 1½" from beginning of 4th R, chain 5, skip next 5 sts, single crochet in next chain-1, continue to work Stitch Pattern. Repeat for other strap.

Bib: Chain 43 with blue yarn. Crochet 14 R in Stitch Pattern, following main Color Sequence.

Finishing: Sew side seams. Sew bib to straps and straps to skirt front, fitting them to your child. Sew on buttons.

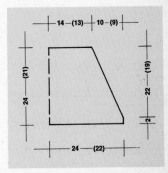

Half-pattern for the largest (smallest) sizes. Numbers are centimeters (10 cm = 4").

Large cushions

Soft, round, and chunky

Sides have a colorful zigzag effect.

Bright patterns made with yarn scraps can be used to make crocheted covers for large round pillows or worn-out leather cushions. See following page for two more patterns.

FOR ALL CUSHIONS

Size: 55 cm diameter x 20 cm high (21$\frac{5}{8}$" diameter x 8" high).

Materials Required:

About 600 gm or 22 oz in a variety of colors. Crochet hook size E.

Basic Stitch: Rounds of single crochet. The first stitch of every round is the turning chain from the previous round. Close every round with a slip stitch into the turning chain.

Tension: 19 sts and 19 rnds = 10 cm or 4".

Abbreviations: St(s) = stitch(es). Rnd(s) = round(s). R = row(s). Dc = double crochet. Sc = single crochet.

HEXAGONAL PATTERN

Work the color pattern shown here, or any sequence of colors desired. Chain 9. Slip stitch into 1st chain to form a ring. Chain 3 to bring work into position for next rnd.

Rnd 1: Work 17 sc into the ring, then chain 3. Rnd 2: Working 2 sc into every 3rd st, sc into each sc of previous rnd – 24 sts. Chain 3 for next rnd. Rnd 3: Working 3 sc into every 4th st, sc into each sc of the previous rnd – 36 sts. Pull piece into hexagonal shape, placing the 3 sc at each corner. Rnd 4: Working 3 sc into the middle sc at corner,

A

B

Different colors and other designs, but they are still chunky, soft, and round.

every R. After 17 R, crochet the last 2 sts together. Repeat for the other sides. Crochet around edges with 4 rnds sc and 2 rnds dc. **Finishing:** Make a length of cord by chaining a double strand of yarn for 2 m or 2 yds. Thread the cord through the last rnd of dc. Place cover over pillow and pull cord tight.

CUSHION A

Work the color pattern shown here, or any sequence of colors desired.

Top: Chain 6. Slip-stitch into 1st chain to form a ring. Chain 3 to begin next rnd. Rnd 1: Work 11 sc into the ring, then chain 3. Rnd 2: Working 2 sc into every 2nd st, sc into each sc of the previous rnd — 18 sts. Rnds 3–13: Continue working sc, adding 6 sc in every rnd — 84 sts. Space the added stitches evenly in the rnd to maintain the circular shape. Rnd 14: Add 11 sts. Rnd 15: Add 6 sts. Rnd 16: Add 11 sts. Rnd 17: Add 25 sts. Rnds 18–21: Work rnds without adding sts. Rnd 22: Add 11 sts. Rnds 23–24: Work rnds without adding sts. Rnd 25: Add 18 sts. Rnds 26–28: Work rnds without adding sts. Rnd 29: Add 25 sts. Rnds 30–36: Work rnds without adding sts. Rnd 37: Add 30 sts. Rnds 38–40: Work rounds without adding sts. Rnd 41: Add 37 sts. Rnds 42–44: Work rnds without adding sts. Rnd 45: Add 30 sts. Rnds 46–48: Work rnds without adding sts. Rnd 49: Add 38 sts — 326 sts. Rnds 50–52: Work rnds without adding sts. Piece should measure 55 cm or 21½". If you wish to make a larger

circle, you must work 1 increase rnd and then 2 rnds without an increase.

Side: The height is 20 cm or 8" plus 8 cm or 3¼" for turn-under. Chain 56. Sc in 4th chain from hook and in each chain across, chain 3, turn. Work across R, starting in 2nd st and ending in the turning chain. The length will depend on the circumference of the pillow. **Finishing:** Sew ends of side together and sew sides to top. Work 2 rnds of dc along the edge. Make a length of cord by chaining a double strand of yarn for 2 m or 2 yds. Thread the cord through the last rnd of dc. Place cover over pillow and pull cord tight.

CUSHION B

Work as for cushion A up to Rnd 48 – 288 sts. Work straight for 38 more rnds. In the following rnd, decrease 15 sts at even intervals – 273 sts. Work straight for the next 5 rnds. Decrease 15 sts in the next rnd – 258 sts. Work straight for 6 more rnds. Work last 2 rnds in dc. **Finishing:** Make a length of cord by chaining a double strand of yarn for 2 m or 2 yds. Thread the cord through the last rnd of dc. Place cover over pillow and pull cord tight.

Hint: You can make the pillow form with sheets of foam rubber. Cut sheets into strips the same width as the cover height. To shape, roll up one strip tightly, then roll another strip around this one, and so on until the circle has the same diameter as the cover. Tie the strips securely in place and fit the cover.

sc into each sc of previous rnd — 48 sts. Repeat rnd 4, working given number of sts into the middle of the corner. Rnds 5–8: 2 sc. Rnd 9: 3 sc. Rnds 10–12: 2 sc. Rnd 13: 3 sc. Rnds 14–16: 2 sc. Rnds 17–20: 3 sc. Rnds 21–23: 2 sc. Rnds 24–27: 3 sc. Rnds 28–30: 2 sc. Rnds 31–32: 3 sc. Rnds 33–39: 2 sc. Rnds 40–50: 3 sc – 462 sts (77 sts on each side). Rnds

51–64: Work 3 sc into each corner. *At the same time,* in each rnd, alternately decrease 2 sts and 3 sts once in the middle of each side. At the end of the 64th rnd there will be 420 sts (70 sts on each side).
Complete each side separately. Fasten yarn in 1 corner and work back and forth across the rows, decreasing 1 st at each end and 2 sts in the middle of

Bright bonnet for baby

A crocheted bonnet can be made very quickly — this one was made in a single afternoon.

The pieces are worked in double crochet, using a different color in every row. Make a random color pattern or try alternating stripes.

A warm head covering is an important item in every baby's wardrobe. This colorful little striped bonnet will keep your baby well protected during its outings. For a change, crochet it in a variety of bright colors, rather than the usual pink or blue.

*

Size: For a baby 6 months to 1 year.

Materials Required:

Leftover yarn in various colors. Crochet hook size E.

Basic Stitch: Double crochet and chain 3 for turning. Every row begins in the 2nd stitch and ends in the turning chain.

Tension: 22 sts and 10 R = 10 cm or 4".

Abbreviations: St(s) = stitch(es). R = row(s). Dc = double crochet. Sc = single crochet.

DIRECTIONS

Front: Chain 36 in any color. Dc in the 2nd chain from the hook and in each chain across, chain 3, turn. Work straight in Basic Stitch for 32 R, or until piece measures 32 cm or $12\frac{5}{8}$". Work every R in a different color and join each new color in the 1st st of the turning chain.

Back: Chain 22 in any color. Dc in the 4th chain from the hook and in each chain across, chain 3, turn. Continue in Basic Stitch, working a new color in every R as before. At 7 cm or $2\frac{3}{4}$", begin to decrease 1 st at each end of every 2nd R 3 times — 14 sts at 13 cm or 5".

Finishing: Sew the Front to the Back. Using 2 strands of yarn, work 1 R of sc around the edges of the bonnet. For the ties, use 3 strands of yarn in the same color as the edging. Make 2 chains, each 40 cm or $15\frac{3}{4}$" long. Sew 1 tie to each corner of the bonnet. For each tassel, cut a piece of yarn about 12 cm or $4\frac{3}{4}$" long in each color. Make 2 bundles and tie each in the middle with yarn in the same color as the ties. Fold the bundles in half and wrap the yarn around the tassels to form a knob. Tie securely. Sew the tassels to the ties.

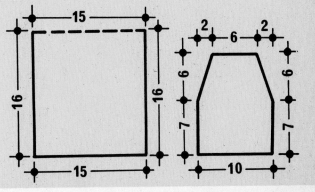

Pattern for back and half-pattern for top. Measurements are in centimeters.

Three great looks in one

This jacket is easy to make because it has very few pieces and can be sewn entirely by hand. It is easy to wear because it is open in front and fits almost everybody! The pattern, which is in three sizes, can be adapted to two different styles. Style 1, shown here in suede, has a seamed back falling from a yoke. Style 2, shown opposite, has a plain yoked back and is more suitable for pile fabrics.

This version features a loose-fitting, seamed back falling from a yoke.

The simple lines
of Style 2 are attractive
in smooth-surfaced,
fake-fur fabric. Or,
make it in a bright,
deep-pile, fake-fur fabric
to wear with casual clothes.

Style 1 in leather

Style 1 of the easy jacket is especially attractive when made up in suede and the seams joined with thonging. Thonged seams are easy to do – a thin strip of leather is threaded through holes punched along the edges of the garment and along the seams. The pattern sheet tells you how to punch the holes and work the thonging.

Style 2 in fake fur

As you will see from the pattern sheet, Style 2 has a plain, unseamed back falling straight from the yoke. This style is simpler and more suitable for bulky fabrics such as fake furs. It is shown here made up in two different types of fake-fur fabric. The white version uses a smooth-surfaced pile which has been finished to look like rabbit fur. The pile of this type of fabric runs one way and the instructions on the pattern sheet regarding pile must be observed.

The pretty red version is in deep-pile fabric, so you need not worry about the direction of the pile.

Instructions for cutting out and sewing fake-fur fabrics are on the pattern sheet. All seams are sewn by hand.

Style 2 in real fur

The pattern sheet includes special instructions for making Style 2 in real fur. There are helpful hints for buying and cutting the skins, sewing the seams, and finishing the edges.

Try it in felt

The simple, clean lines of the pattern are also effective when made up in felt.

Felt is available in a wide range of colors and is easy to sew. Both Styles 1 and 2 are suitable for felt and you can use the basic hand stitches and seams.

When you've finished, try decorating your felt jacket with bright yarn embroidery or stick-on patches.

Pattern is in 3 sizes

Size A: bust 80 cm (31½").
Size B: bust 84 cm (33").
Size C: bust 88 cm (34½").
(For Size D, bust 92 cm [36"], use Size C pattern.)

Basic hand-sewn seams and finishes

The Illustrated Sewing, which begins here, will take you through a complete dressmaking course from the basic stitches and seams to more complicated sewing techniques. The lessons will help you make the featured designs and will be a handy reference as you progress through the course. More experienced dressmakers will also find these pages an invaluable review, enabling them to perfect familiar techniques.

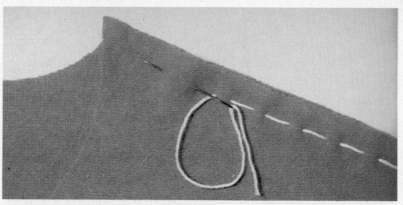

Basting Stitch: Basting is a temporary stitch used to hold two or more pieces of fabric together until final stitching. It is also used to indicate guidelines. It is worked in a contrasting color. To baste, pass the needle in and out of the fabric, making a long stitch on the upper side and a shorter one on the underside. The upper stitches are about 1 cm ($\frac{1}{2}$″).

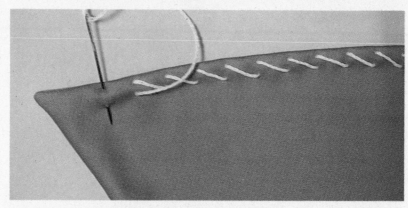

Diagonal Basting: This stitch is used to hold layers of fabric together firmly. It will secure the sections of a garment during fitting, pressing, edge-stitching, etc. Stitch through the layers of fabric at right angles to the edge. This makes a long diagonal stitch on the upper side and a short vertical stitch on the underside.

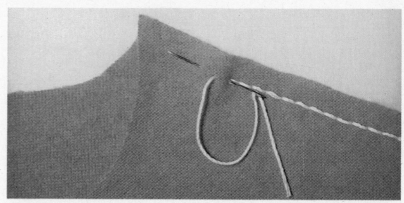

Backstitch: Backstitching is used to stitch a seam permanently by hand. To begin, bring thread through to right side of fabric. Place needle in fabric one stitch length (0.5 cm or $\frac{3}{16}$″) back and bring it out one stitch length ahead of the thread. The seam looks like machine-stitching on the upper side and the stitches overlap on the underside.

60

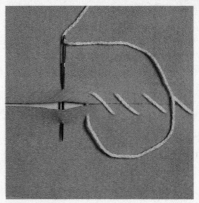

Overcasting: This stitch is used on the raw edges of fabrics to keep them from raveling. Work from left to right and insert the needle into the fabric from back to front, holding the needle at an angle so that the stitches lie diagonally. Stitches should be worked close together and evenly, but do not pull the thread too tightly.

Flat joining: This stitch is used to join abutting, non-fraying materials such as leather and felt. It is similar to diagonal basting, and worked from right to left.

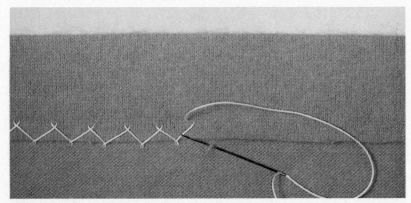

Slip Stitch: Slip stitch is used for hems or in places where the stitching should not show. The stitches are worked diagonally and fairly loosely. Make a small stitch through the top fabric, picking up only two or three threads, and then make a stitch under two or three threads of the under fabric. Make stitches 0.5 cm ($\frac{1}{8}''-\frac{1}{4}''$) apart.

Many home sewers have sewing machines and these can make sewing jobs far easier and pleasanter. However, in dressmaking, a certain amount of hand sewing is required. Fragile fabrics sometimes require hand-sewn seams and intricate corners or edges may need to be hand stitched. In fact, hand sewing is essential to good dressmaking and a hand-sewn detail can give a garment that special, professional-looking quality which is unmistakable. For this reason, this first lesson in Illustrated Sewing shows how the basic hand-sewn seams and stitches are worked.

They are not difficult to master and once you have accustomed yourself to using needle and thread, you will see how easy it is to sew. In a short time, you will be making simple clothes – even if you do not have a sewing machine. The jackets illustrated on the previous pages were made entirely by hand and your efforts will look just as professional.

You will find more dressmaking how-to on the pattern sheet itself. This is part of the Illustrated Sewing course and even if you do not intend to make the jacket immediately, you will find that your knowledge of dressmaking will be increased just by reading through the instructions.

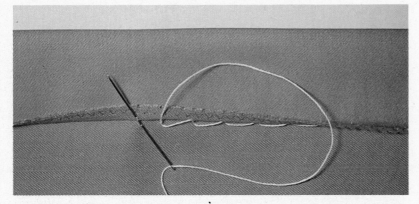

Herringbone or Catch Stitch: This is used to secure the raw edges of facings and interfacings. Work from left to right. Take a small stitch through the upper fabric, inserting the needle from right to left, then a small stitch through the under fabric, inserting the needle from right to left. The threads will cross each other as shown.

Be casual and comfortable

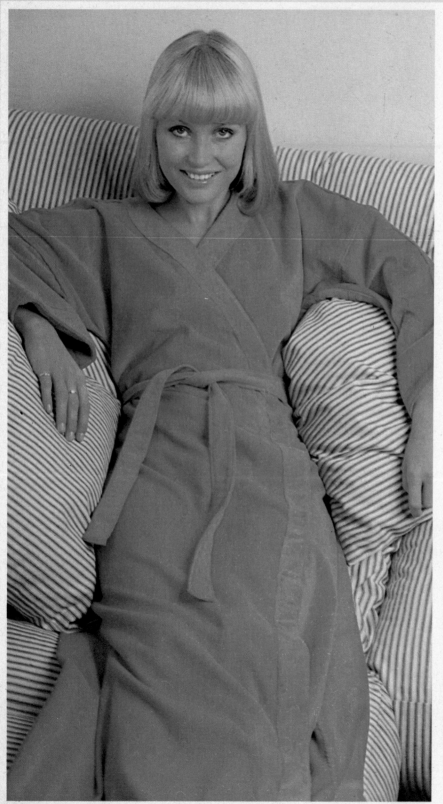

Call it whatever you like — dressing gown, bathrobe, or housecoat — you will always look good in it. You can wear it while relaxing at home or when dashing off for a day at the beach. The long style is made of velour, and the short one is made of toweling. Both are easy-care fabrics and can be machine-washed. Sizes B and D are on the pattern sheet; sizes A, C, and E can be adapted. (See Body Measurements Chart on pattern sheet.)

Soft cotton velour was used for the long version. The edging can be made with the wrong side out for texture contrast.

The garment is made with flat-fell seams. To avoid a bulge where two flat-fell seams meet, cut away part of one seam allowance, close to the stitching line (see illustrations at right). This will enable the upper seam to be "counter sunk" into the lower seam. Machine-stitch slowly where two flat-fell seams meet to avoid breaking the needle.

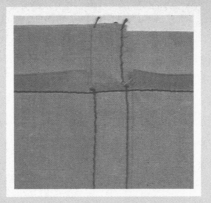 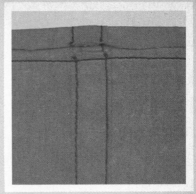

The short version was made up in toweling. The band has been omitted from this style and the edges finished with cotton braid. A patch pocket has been added.

Sewing with a machine

When you buy a sewing machine, you get a book of instructions which explains how to operate it. You should study these instructions carefully, because by knowing your machine really well, you will get the best out of it. See the opposite page for additional tips about what to do when something goes wrong.

The seams and seam finishes shown on these pages are the basic machine-stitching techniques for a variety of types and weights of fabrics.

Plain Seam

Stitching a plain seam
Raise the presser foot and place the basted or pinned fabric under the needle, exactly in line with the intended seam. Lower the needle into the fabric, then lower the presser foot. Guide the fabric through the machine with the fingertips held near the presser foot. Do not pull the fabric through the machine.

Beginning and ending a seam
a. Begin about 2.5 cm (1") from edge and stitch back to edge, then stitch forward for the seam. At the end, reverse the machine and take several stitches back over the stitches of the seam.
b. Cut the threads, leaving enough thread to tie a double square knot. This method is used when sewing finer fabrics.

Seam finishing

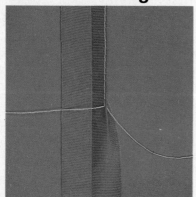

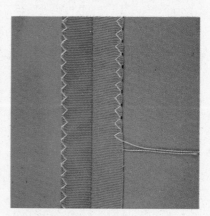

Making a stitched edge
Clothes last longer if seams are finished. For non-bulky fabrics, press the seam open and turn raw edges under 0.5 cm ($\frac{1}{4}$"). Machine-stitch along the fold, stitching only through the seam allowance.
Note: When pressing the seams, place a strip of brown paper between the seam allowance and the garment to prevent a mark on the right side of the fabric.

Making a zigzag edge
Swing needle sewing machines have a zigzag stitch which can be used for fabrics of all weights. Press the seam open and trim the edges neatly. Guide the seam allowance under the foot so stitching is close to the raw edge. Stitch only through the seam allowance. The stitch depth and width should be adjusted according to the weave of the fabric.

Making a double-edge finish
This type of finishing is used on fine fabrics. Press the seam allowance to one side and trim the edges neatly. Work zigzag stitch through both layers of the seam allowance together.
Note: Zigzag stitching can also be used for seaming stretch fabrics, making simple buttonholes, attaching decorative edgings, and working quick appliqué.

Know your sewing machine
What to do when...

Flat-fell seam

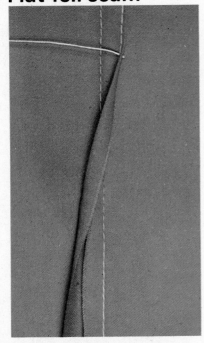

Making a flat-fell seam
The flat-fell seam is used on sportswear, children's clothes, and garments which are likely to receive a great deal of wear and washing. The seam looks neat on the inside of the garment as well as the outside and no extra finishing is required.

First, pin or baste the pieces, wrong sides together, and stitch a plain seam. Press the seam allowance to one side. Trim the lower seam allowance to 0.5cm ($\frac{1}{4}$″). Turn under raw edge of the upper seam allowance, fold it over trimmed edge, and pin or baste in place, making sure that the seam is the same width all the way down. Top-stitch along the folded edge, working through all thicknesses of the fabric.

Making a hemmed-fell seam
This seam is similar to the flat-fell seam, but makes a less conspicuous finish on the right side. Work as for flat-felled seam, but slip-stitch by hand along fold, making tiny stitches.

... the upper thread breaks
a. the machine is threaded incorrectly – check the manufacturer's instruction book for proper threading of the machine.
b. the needle is bent or crooked – change the needle.
c. poor quality or dried-out thread – try newer thread.

... the needle breaks
a. the needle screw is not sufficiently tightened – tighten it.
b. the needle is bent and is hitting the needle plate – replace it.
c. the material is too thick – try a stronger needle.

... the fabric threads are pulled
a. the needle point is blunt or broken – change the needle.
b. the needle size is too coarse for the fabric – change to a smaller needle size.

... the thread frays
a. the needle is too fine for the thread – change to a larger size.
b. poor quality thread – change to better quality thread.

... the stitching isn't even
a. the bobbin is unevenly wound – check the manufacturer's instruction book for proper bobbin winding method.
b. the cardboard spool is crushed and the spool does not turn freely. Put a small round of felt under the spool.

... the fabric isn't being taken through the machine
a. there is dust between the teeth of the feed – pick out the dust particles very carefully. If the machine is used frequently, this cleaning will have to be done fairly often.

... the machine will not sew
sewing thread has become wound around the bobbin holder and the bobbin will not turn –
1. cut the thread and pull out the thread which is caught.
2. move the wheel back and forth to release the piece of thread.

...you have to stop in mid-sew
if you are interrupted in your work, stop the machine, leaving the needle point in the work.

... the seam is crinkling
upper and lower tensions are too tight – check the manufacturer's instructions regarding tensions.

... stitches are looping
a. upper tension is too loose and lower tension is too tight – the top thread is being pulled to the underside.
b. or the situation is reversed and the bobbin thread is being pulled through, causing knots to form. With a piece of scrap fabric in machine, adjust upper and lower tension until the stitch is being correctly worked and looks the same on both sides of the fabric. Tension is usually altered by a small adjustment of the tension guide on the machine (check the manufacturer's instructions regarding tensions).

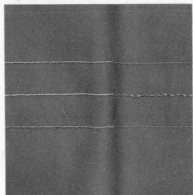

... adjusting thread tension
These lines show the results of correct and incorrect tension. The top thread is shown at left and the bobbin thread is shown at the right of the photograph. Top: The upper and lower tensions match. Middle: Lower tension is too tight. Knots are being formed on the underside. Bottom: The upper tension is too tight. Knots are being formed on top.

The long and short of it

Every wardrobe needs a classic skirt. This one has a back zipper to assure a smooth fit on the hips, and a gentle flare for graceful movement. Sizes B and D are given on the pattern sheet and sizes A, C, and E can be adapted from the pattern (see pattern sheet for Measurements Chart).

To give a smart look to plain or tweed fabric, add squared patch pockets with crisp top-stitched detailing.

This tweed classic is just right for a casual knitted pullover.

Patch pockets can be made with the top edges cut away for a very hip-slimming line. Finish the edges with top-stitching.

Elegantly styled skirt looks superb with a classic silk shirt.

A long skirt is feminine and comfortable, and it's not any more trouble to make than a short one. In fact, both the long and short versions are made from the same pattern.

Long skirts are easy to pack and they are fashion news all year round, so why not make one in a pretty floral cotton print for romantic strolls along the beach next summer? For winter holidays or après-ski, make another skirt in a quilted fabric or a colorful wool plaid. If you prefer to make the skirt in a plain fabric, add sporty patch pockets and top-stitched detailing as shown on the short tweed skirts, opposite.

Inserting a zipper

There are several ways of inserting zippers into garments. This method is used in seams, at necklines, sleeves, and in center front or center back of garments. While zippers can be sewn by hand, skirt and pants zippers are generally stitched by machine because of the amount of stress they receive.

1 Stitch seam to the point where zipper begins; fasten threads. Finish seam with machine or hand-basted stitches. Press the seam open, running the tip of the iron under the seam allowances to remove pressing marks.

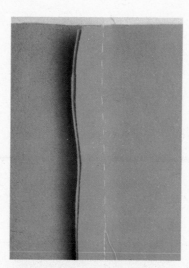

2 With the right side of the skirt up, open the zipper and lay it along the basted seam so that the teeth of one side of the zipper are on the seam line. Pin, then baste this side of the zipper, using diagonal basting stitch. Close the zipper and baste the other side. The zipper should lie flat and taut.

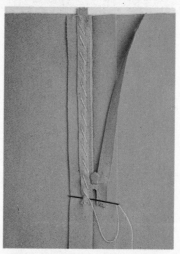

3 Attach the zipper foot to the machine. Stitch down one side of the zipper, being careful to stitch an even distance from the teeth so the stitching line will be straight on the right side. Stitch to the end of the zipper, then, with the needle in the fabric, lift the foot and pivot the fabric so you can stitch across the bottom of the zipper. Lower foot and stitch across zipper. At the other side, pivot the fabric again and stitch up to waist. Remove all basting stitches.

Note: To keep stitching lines even, do not stitch next to the zipper pull. Unzip for about 5 cm (2"), stitch down to the pull, close the zipper again, and resume stitching.

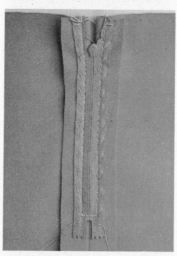

Attaching a waistband

1 Fold the waistband in half lengthwise, wrong sides together, and press the fold. Open the fabric and place the interfacing along the fold 1 cm ($\frac{1}{2}$") from right edge as shown. Machine-stitch along the fold-line edge of the interfacing. Finish the edge on this half of the waistband with zigzag stitching.

2 Fold back the waistband, right sides together, and stitch across both ends. Cut diagonally across the corners at the fold edge so the corners will lie flat. Turn the skirt to the wrong side. Match the waistband to the skirt waist, right sides together, placing the unfinished edge of the waistband along the skirt edge and making the waistband flush with the right edge of the zipper. (The flush edge of the skirt will be at the left when the skirt is turned right side out.) Let the remainder of the waistband extend beyond the skirt at the other side.

Place pins at right angles to the seam line as shown. Pin at the side seams, center front, and center back, then pin the spaces in between. Baste and stitch.

The waistband should be cut to your waist
measurement, plus 6 cm (2½″) for ease, seam allowance,
and overlap. The depth should be twice that
of the band desired, plus 3 cm (1¼″) for seam allowance.

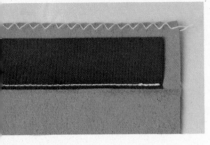

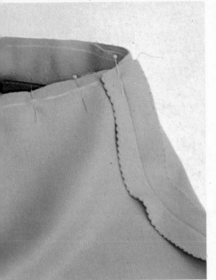

4 Turn the skirt right side out. Make sharp, neat corners by picking out the corners of the waistband with a straight pin.
Tip: Baste loops of bias seam tape to the inside of the waist seam for skirt hangers.

5 Pin the waistband in place. To avoid excessive thickness, do not turn in the finished edge. Stitch waistband exactly on the seam line on the right side, stitching through the waistband fabric on the wrong side of the skirt.

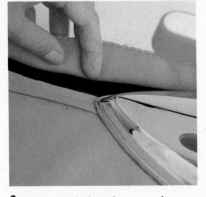

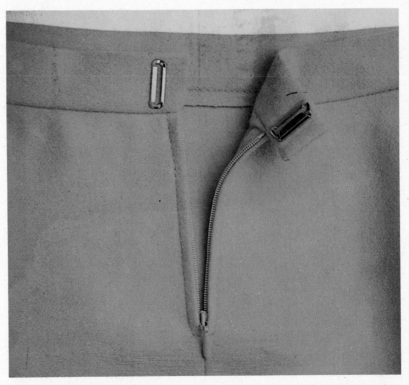

3 Turn waistband up and press open the seam allowance. Place the unstitched edge of the interfacing behind the waistband seam allowance. Trim the skirt seam allowance to 1 cm (⅜″) to reduce the bulk of the many layers of fabric at the seam.

6 Turn in the raw edges along the bottom of the waistband overlap and slip-stitch the opening closed. Sew a skirt hook and bar to the overlap and waistband. If the fastener shown here is not available, substitute two small hooks and eyes. Remove basting stitches.

Tailoring: How to begin

Tailoring is a building and molding process, and pants are a good place to begin. Pants are an important part of the fashion scene because they can be worn for daytime or evening and they are appropriate for occasions ranging from the ultra casual to the very elegant. To look smart, pants must fit properly. The advantage of making pants yourself is that you can adjust them to your body contours and achieve a comfortable and flattering fit.

The pattern sheet explains how to fit and construct these basic pants, and the illustrated lesson covering darts and pants zippers will be a help.

Sizes C and E are given on the pattern sheet. Sizes B, D, and F can be adapted from the pattern. See the Body Measurements Chart and choose the proper pattern size by matching your hip measurement. If your waist measurement is not the same as the one on the chart, the pattern can be easily adjusted.

The pants hang long and straight from the hips. This is a flattering line which can be used to camouflage heavy thighs. Color, too, can have a significant influence on the total effect of your pants. Warm colors can increase the apparent size of your figure, while cool colors make it appear smaller.

Sporty or dressy?

The pattern can be made up in a wide variety of fabrics, depending upon whether you want a sporty or dressy look. The two versions shown here are in gaberdine and denim.

Large patch pockets and top-stitched details on the seams, waistband, pockets, and belt loops add to the informality of the denim.

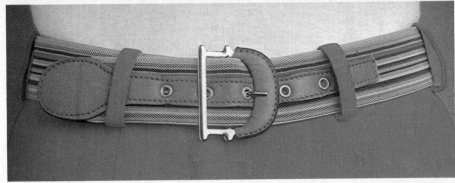

Belt loops are stitched on with the waistband. Two lines of top-stitching may be added if desired.

Here is how your pants should look from behind – no strain on the seam, no crease marks, and no bagginess.

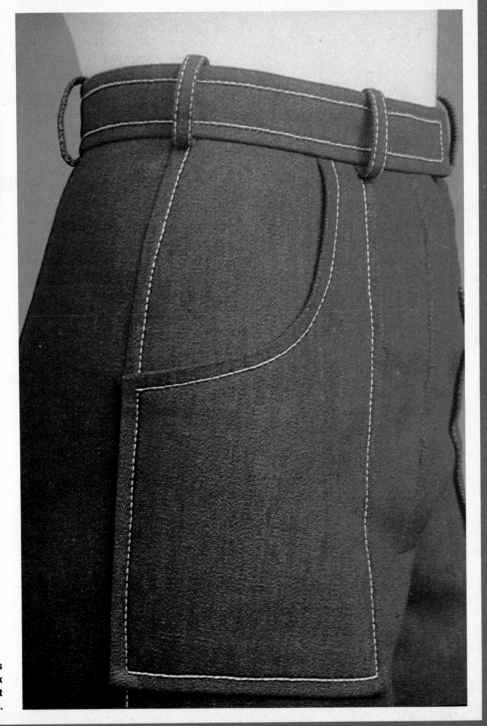

The heavy white top-stitching gives lively detailing to denim jeans. Work white outlines around pockets, belt loops, and waistband or along seams.

Making a dart

Darts are used to shape the flat fabric to the rounded contours of the body. Darts are designed for an average height, so you may have to adjust them slightly to conform to your height. A short figure requires shorter darts and a tall figure requires longer darts.

1 Darts must be marked very precisely on the fabric so that they are an even distance from the seams and an even length. Mark them with dressmaker's tracing paper or tailor's tacks as shown above. Make a short horizontal line with the tracing paper and tracing wheel or thread to mark the end of the dart.

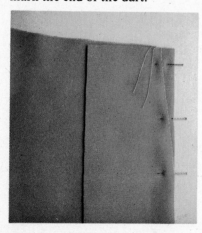

2 Fold the fabric, right sides together, matching line markings. Pin the fabric in place.

3 Darts are basted from the point to the wide end and stitched from the wide end to the point. In this way, you can hold the fabric more easily in basting and make a more precise point when stitching. The last two or three stitches should be made directly on the fold to eliminate a tuck at the point. Secure the threads with a knot to avoid an unsightly pucker or bubble.

Note: Not all darts are straight. The styling of many designs require concave or convex curves. Stitch carefully along the lines to keep the proper curve.

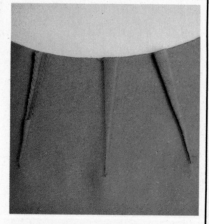

Three ways to press darts
●Deep darts or darts in heavy fabric should be cut down the fold line to within 2.5 cm (1″) of the point. Press the dart open and overcast the raw edges.
●Press the dart flat with the seam in the center.
●Press the dart to one side. Vertical darts should be pressed toward center front or back. Horizontal darts should be pressed downward.
Always stitch darts before stitching major seams or before intersecting them with seams. Press darts over a tailor's ham to maintain the curved contour created by the dart.

Fly front placket for pants

This is a technique for putting a zipper into a seam which follows a body curve. It is usually used for the center front of pants, and occasionally on jackets and coats. You may use a specially constructed pants zipper or use a regular zipper, depending on the weight of the fabric to be used.

You will probably have to shorten the zipper, and the pattern sheet tells what zipper length to use for each size. Be careful to allow sufficient seam allowance for the insertion of the zipper (3 cm or $1\frac{1}{8}″$) into the seam.

This is also the technique to use when the zipper breaks in a favorite pair of pants. There is no need to throw away the pants when there is a simple way to replace the zipper. Even novice tailors will find this an easy and successful method.

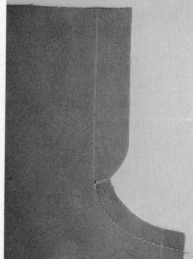

1 A wider seam allowance (3 cm or $1\frac{1}{4}″$) is added for the zipper. Mark point where the zipper will end and round off the corner of the wider seam allowance. With the fabric pieces right sides together, stitch the crotch seam up to the mark. Secure the seam with backstitches.

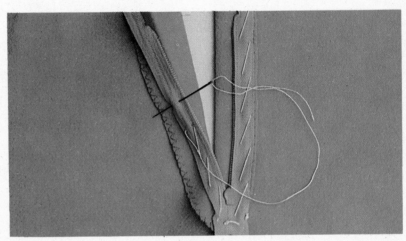

2 Clip the seam allowance at the mark at the top of the crotch seam. Mark the seam line on each side with basting stitches. With the right side up, fold back the seam at the right edge so the fold is 0.5 cm ($\frac{1}{4}''$) beyond the seamline. Press. At the left edge, fold and press where marked. Remove the basting threads.

Pressing Hints
Always press with a cloth between the iron and the fabric. Raise and lower the iron with a gentle motion so that you don't distort the grain of the fabric. Place brown paper between the seam allowance and the fabric to avoid marks on right side of fabric.

4 Open the zipper and place it face down on the wrong side of the opening. Place the zipper teeth along the fold at the left edge and the right side 0.5 cm ($\frac{3}{8}''$) from the fold so the fabric will lie flat when the zipper is closed. Baste in place with diagonal basting. If the zipper is too long, let the excess extend beyond the pants at the top edge.

curve at the bottom corner and stitching straight across the bottom to the fold. Because the base of the opening is subject to strain, strengthen with extra stitches.

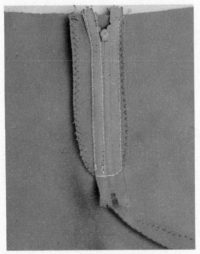

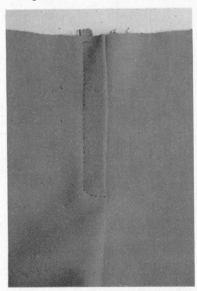

3 Finish all raw edges with zig-zag stitch. Remember to finish the clipped edges as well as the zipper and crotch seams.

5 Using a zipper foot attachment, stitch the left side of the zipper close to the teeth edge. Make a second line of stitching along the edge of the tape, about 0.5 cm ($\frac{1}{4}''$) away from the first line of stitching, being careful not to stitch beyond overlap. Close the zipper. Make sure the fold of the overlap forms a continuous line with the crotch seam. Stitch the right side, making a

6 Remove all basting threads and press from the right side. Trim ends of zipper even with upper edge of the pants if necessary.

Quick and easy toymaking

From Mother, with love

Children like large stuffed animals which they can hug and toss about. Why not make a beguiling teddy bear or panda of soft, warm fake-fur fabric? The pattern and directions are so simple, you can make these charming cuddle-toys very quickly.

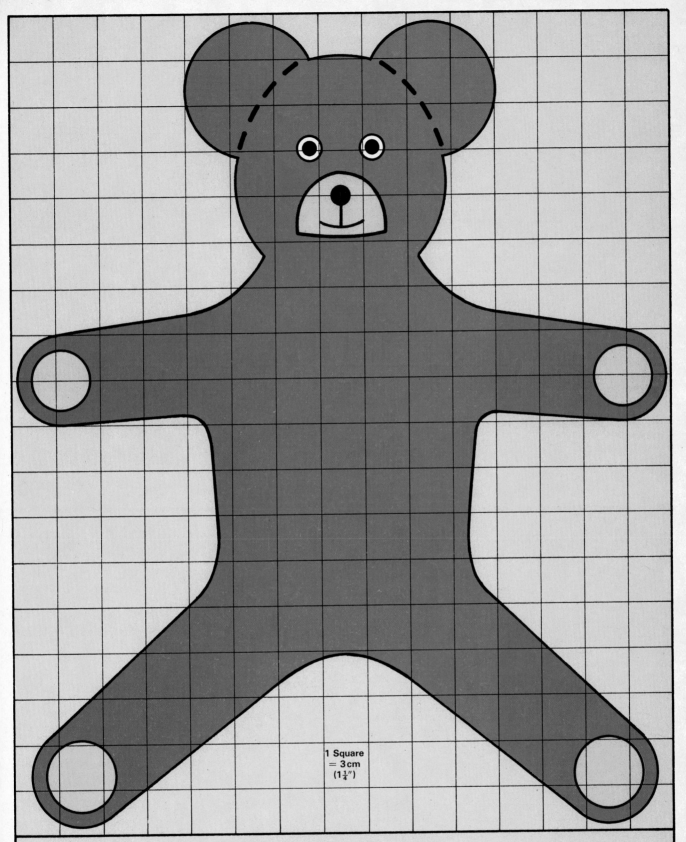

1 Square
= 3 cm
(1¼")

Enlarging a graph pattern

A graph pattern is simply a plan from which you draw your own paper pattern. The scale of the pattern here is 1 square = 3 cm (1¼"). To make a pattern for the bear, draw an area 45 cm x 54 cm (18¾" x 22½") on a piece of paper and mark it off into 3 cm (1¼") squares. Make dots where the bear outline touches the lines of the graph. Connect the dots and your pattern is ready to use. Any pattern can be enlarged by putting a grid over it and redrawing it on larger squares.

Size: 53 cm (21″) tall.

Materials Required:

Teddy Bear: Brown fake-fur fabric 70 cm x 140 cm wide (27″ x 54″ wide). Lightweight brown corduroy 10 cm x 45 cm (4″ x 18″). Small pieces of white and black felt. 2 stuffed-toy eyes. 1 small black dome button. Brown sewing thread. Foam pieces for stuffing. **Panda:** White fake-fur fabric 70 cm x 140 cm wide (27″ x 54″ wide). Black fake-fur fabric 23 cm x 90 cm (9″ x 36″). Lightweight black corduroy 10 cm x 36 cm (4″ x 14″). 2 stuffed-toy eyes. White and black sewing thread. Foam pieces for stuffing.

Making the teddy bear

Both the teddy bear and panda are made from a graph pattern. Follow enlarging instructions under graph to make the pattern.

1. Fold fabric in half, right sides together, making sure pile runs downward on both halves. Pin pattern in place and trace outline onto the fabric with tailor's chalk.

2. Baste fabric together so pieces won't shift. Cut out, adding 2 cm ($\frac{3}{4}$″) seam allowance around edge. Stitch on chalked line, leaving 10 cm (4″) open at crotch for stuffing. (If sewing by hand, use backstitch on all seams.)

3. Trim seam allowance to 1 cm ($\frac{3}{8}$″). Clip all corners and curves to stitching. Turn teddy bear to the right side.

4. Stuff with foam. Turn edges of opening to inside and slip-stitch closed.

Paws: Cut paw pads from pattern. Trace onto wrong side of corduroy. Cut out, adding 1 cm ($\frac{3}{8}$″) seam allowance. Work small running stitches on chalked line. Clip seam allowance to stitching and turn to wrong side on thread outline. Baste seam allowance in place. Sew paw pads to legs.

Face: Cut muzzle from pattern and trace onto wrong side of corduroy, adding

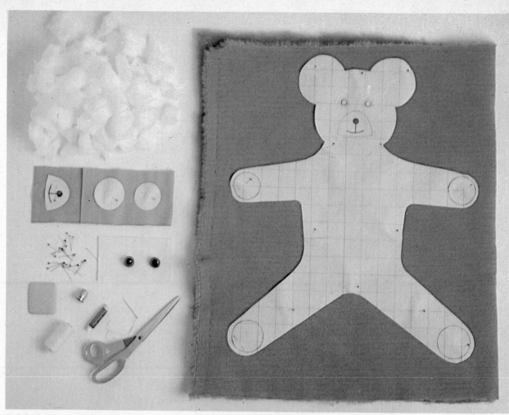

1. Fold fabric, right sides together. Pin pattern to the fabric and mark outline with tailor's chalk. Mark pads and muzzle.

2. Remove the pattern. Baste fabric together. Stitch on chalked outlines.

3. Cut out bear. Clip seam allowance to the stitching line along curves.

4. Stuff bear, making sure the ears and legs are well filled and joints are loose.

seam allowance as for pads. Cut mouth from black felt; stitch to muzzle. Sew on nose button. Make muzzle in same manner as paw pads and sew to face, leaving bottom open for stuffing. Stuff and sew opening closed. Cut two outer eye circles from white felt and secure in place with eyes.

Making the panda

Mark pattern on white fake-fur fabric as for teddy bear, but omit the ears. Mark and cut ears from black fake-fur fabric, adding 1 cm ($\frac{3}{8}$″) seam allowance. Baste body pieces together, but leave head unbasted. Stitch two ears to each head piece, right sides together. Fold up ears, baste head, and complete as for teddy bear. Make paw pads from corduroy and muzzle from fake-fur fabric. Mouth and nose are omitted. Secure eyes, but omit felt.

Running Stitch: Pass the needle over and under the fabric to make a line of stitches. The stitches are usually an even length.

76

Moccasins in sheepskin and suede

Warm your toes in a pair of soft and comfortable moccasins. Easy to make, they are ideal gifts for friends and family. These are made of sheepskin, leather, and suede, but leather and fake-fur fabric would be just as effective.

Materials Required:
Suede for sides. Leather for soles. Sheepskin for tops. Heavy-duty thread. Leather needle or, for machine stitching, a leather machine-needle. A leather punch with several cutting surfaces. Leather glue. Cardboard for the patterns.

Making the moccasins
Pattern pieces are for the right foot, and these should be reversed for the left foot. Trace the pattern pieces onto stiff paper or lightweight cardboard with dressmaker's carbon paper. Join the pieces marked 3 along the short edges

Trace the moccasin pattern below or use it as a guide for adapting other sizes

with tape. Lay the pattern pieces on the fabric as follows. Place piece 3 (sides) onto the wrong side of the suede. Draw around shape with a pencil. Cut out these pieces for right and left feet. Repeat for sole pattern and leather. Place pattern piece 2 onto the wrong side of the sheepskin; draw around the shape and cut out two tops, being careful to cut only the backing and not the fleece. Mark all the dots, holes, numerals, and letters on the wrong side of the pieces. Punch out the larger holes where indicated. Then, using the smaller hole on the punch, cut out where marked on the sides and the tops. Join the ends of the side pieces by overlapping on the dotted line. Machine-stitch or backstitch by hand along both edges for a neat, flat seam. With wrong sides facing, match the points on the sides marked A, B, and C with those on the sole. Stitch or overcast the edges with heavy-duty thread. With wrong sides facing, match the points marked 1, 2, 3, and 4 on the tops to those marked on the sides and stitch the edges.

Glue a narrow strip of leather over all seams on the right side. Finally, cut leather thongs and overcast all around the sides through the large holes.

If the moccasins are to be made from fake-fur fabric, add 1 cm ($\frac{3}{8}''$) seam allowance on all pieces. Make as for leather moccasins, with seams on inside. You can also make the pattern in felt, embroidering a design on the tops with brightly colored wools.

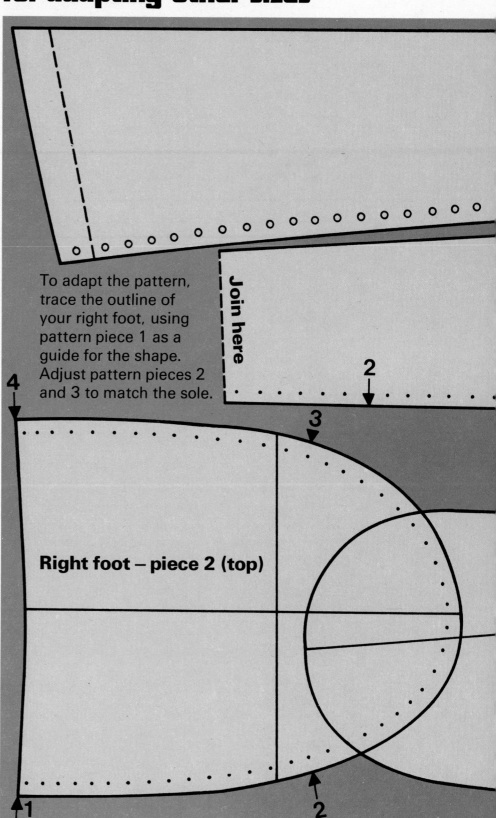

To adapt the pattern, trace the outline of your right foot, using pattern piece 1 as a guide for the shape. Adjust pattern pieces 2 and 3 to match the sole.

Join here

Right foot – piece 2 (top)

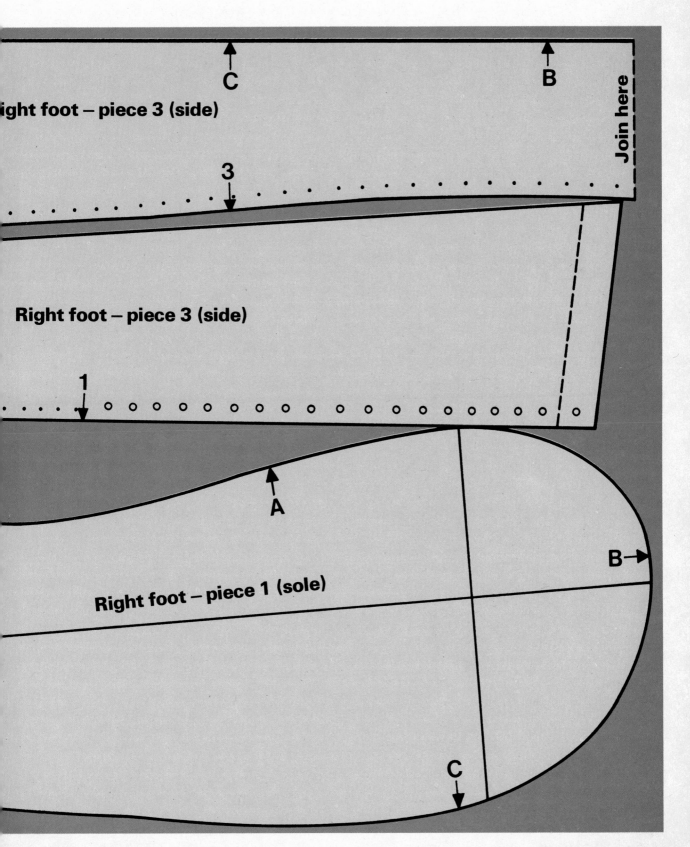

ight foot – piece 3 (side)

C

B

Join here

3

Right foot – piece 3 (side)

1

A

Right foot – piece 1 (sole)

B

C

Kitchen curtains in

Barber pole stripes

The finished size of *each* curtain of the pair should be the same as the height by the width of the area to be covered (this allows for fullness when the curtain is closed). Make a diagram of the two curtain halves, side by side, so the stripes will be continuous when the curtains are pulled across the window. Enlarge the diagram to actual size and make tissue paper pattern pieces, adding 1 cm ($\frac{3}{8}$") seam allowance, 2 cm ($\frac{3}{4}$") for sides and top, and 4 cm ($1\frac{1}{2}$") for hem at bottom. To determine the amount of fabric required for

each color, arrange strips side by side and end to end to work out the most economical width and length of fabric to use. Pin pieces along the lengthwise threads of the fabric and cut out the strips. With right sides

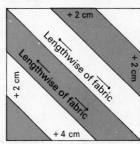

together, pin and stitch the strips. Finish all raw seam allowance edges with zigzag stitch. Press seam allowances toward the darker color.

Turn in allowance at side edges, turn under raw edge,

Plan the curtains carefully before beginning. Draw diagrams of the curtains side by side so the stripes will be continuous when the curtains are closed.

and stitch in place. Caution! The fabric is cut on the bias along the outside edges, so don't stretch the fabric when stitching. Turn in allowances at top and bottom as for sides and stitch in place. If you wish to gather the curtains along the top, cut two pieces of elastic or bias tape which measure a little more than half the width of each curtain half. Pull one piece through the casing formed at the top of each curtain half and stitch to curtain half at each end. Arrange gathers evenly and sew on curtain rings.

Cushions and a quilt
in patchwork and appliqué

Sewing

Mix and match patterns in black and white

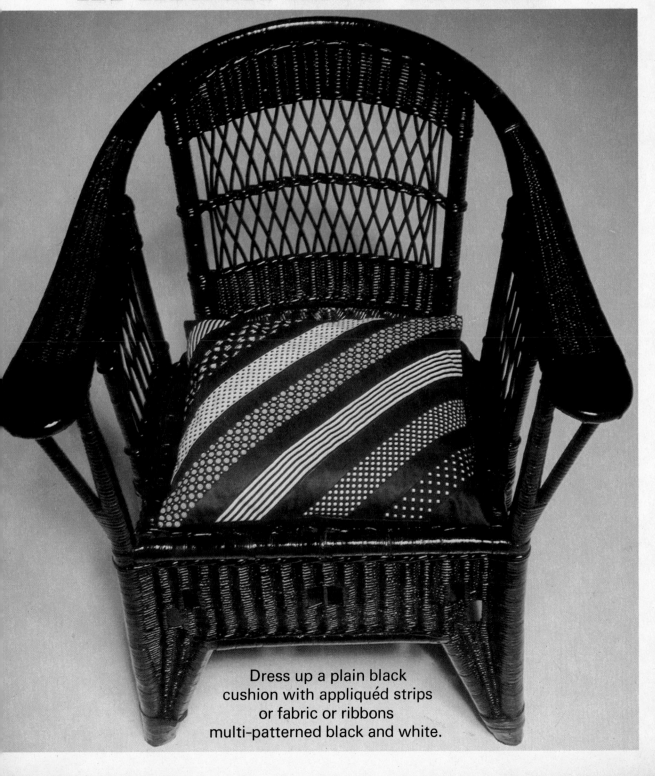

Dress up a plain black
cushion with appliquéd strips
or fabric or ribbons
multi-patterned black and white.

81

Sewing

Transform an old coverlet into a smashing patchwork quilt! Piece together squares from as many black-and-white fabrics as you can find, then sew the patchwork top to the coverlet. Add a patterned backing fabric and the quilt is finished. Extend the black-and-white theme to a circle cushion made of wedges in alternating light and dark patterns.

PATCHWORK CIRCLE

Draw a circle the size of your pillow. Fold the paper in half, then quarters, then eighths. Cut out one of the segments for a pattern, adding 1 cm ($\frac{3}{8}$″) seam allowance. Cut eight segments out of different fabrics. Join pieces to make four pairs. Join pairs to make two halves, then join the halves. Cut out backing the same size as pieced circle and join the pillow pieces, right sides together, leaving 15 cm (6″) open. Turn to right side, insert pillow, and slip-stitch closed. Edge with cording if desired.

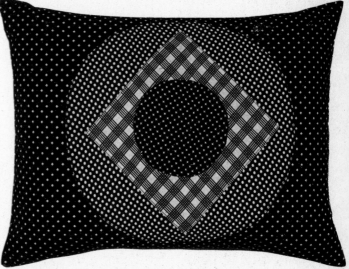

Build pattern on pattern in appliqués for a stunning complement to the quilt.

Materials Required: Pillows. An old coverlet. Fabrics: assorted remnants of black and white cotton prints; large piece of fabric for backing for each. Black sewing thread.

PATCHWORK COVER

Measure your quilt and divide the area into squares. Our coverlet is made up of 23 cm (9″) squares. Cut a cardboard template the size of the finished square, plus 1 cm ($\frac{3}{8}$″) seam allowance. Cut out required number of squares, using the template. Machine-stitch the squares into strips; press all seams to one side. Stitch the strips together and press. Place patchwork piece over coverlet, right sides up, and hand-sew to coverlet, sewing through patchwork and coverlet along all the seam lines. Place the backing on the patchwork, right sides together, and machine-stitch around three sides. Turn right side out and slip-stitch the opening closed.

APPLIQUÉ PILLOW

Cut two pillow pieces. Cut a large circle of contrasting fabric, adding 0.5 cm ($\frac{1}{4}$″) seam allowance. Appliqué circle in the center of one pillow piece. Cut a square to fit inside the circle and a smaller circle to fit in the square. Appliqué the small circle in the square, then the square in the large circle. Place pillow pieces right sides together and stitch around three sides. Turn right side out and insert pillow. Slip-stitch closed.

Appliquéing

Lightly mark the pattern on background fabric. Mark pattern outline on the fabric, then mark a 0.5 cm ($\frac{1}{4}$″) seam allowance all around. Machine or hand-stitch on the design outline for a neat turning edge. Cut out piece along seam allowance outline. Clip all corners and curves. Turn in seam allowance just inside the stitching line and press. Slip-stitch to background.

1   2   3   4

Persian patterns in cross-stitch

Cross-stitch is one of the oldest embroidery stitches known. For hundreds of years, it has been used for decorating furnishings and clothes in Europe, North Africa, and in the Middle East. The five belts here are based on Persian patterns and are so simple to work that you can follow them even if you have never tried canvaswork before.

Directions for working cross-stitch on canvas are shown on the following pages.

A canvaswork belt looks smart when it is worn with a plain pullover and pants.

Basic stitch: Cross-stitch over two canvas meshes.

Belt 1
Size: 4.5 cm (1¾") wide.
Materials Required: Canvas: 11 or 12 meshes to 2.5 cm (1"). Tapestry yarn: 2 skeins beige and 1 skein each of black, scarlet, red-brown, pink. Buckle. Belt backing. Sewing thread.

Belt 2
Size: 4 cm (1⅝") wide.
Materials Required: Canvas: 14 meshes to 2.5 cm (1"). Tapestry yarn: 5 skeins scarlet, 2 skeins black, 1 skein beige. Buckle. Belt backing. Sewing thread.

Belt 3
Size: 6 cm (2¼") wide.
Materials Required: Canvas: 11 or 12 meshes to 2.5 cm (1"). Tapestry yarn: 3 skeins beige, 1 skein each of scarlet, pink, black, red-brown. Buckle. Belt backing. Sewing thread.

Belt 4
Size: 4 cm (1⅝") wide.
Materials Required: Canvas: 14 meshes to 2.5 cm (1"). Tapestry yarn: 5 skeins black, 2 skeins scarlet, 1 skein beige. Buckle. Belt backing. Sewing thread.

Belt 5
Size: 4 cm (1⅝") wide.
Materials Required: Canvas: 14 meshes to 2.5 cm (1"). Tapestry yarn: 5 skeins beige, 1 skein each of red and black. Buckle. Belt backing. Sewing thread.

Estimating canvas
Measure the waist and add 30 cm (12") for overlap,

5

seam allowance, and sewing on the buckle. To determine the width, note the belt width given and add 10 cm (4″) seam allowance. **Note:** Use a buckle with no prong and make sure the cross bar of the buckle is slightly larger than the finished belt width.

Working the cross-stitch

Tape or overcast the raw edges of the canvas to prevent fraying. Begin the embroidery at a corner 5 cm (2″) in from both edges. Follow illustrations for pattern and colors. Be careful to cross all stitches in the same direction. First, work one row of crosses around edges of belt as an outline, then fill in the pattern.

Making the belt

Trim the canvas edges to 2 cm (¾″) and cut away excess canvas at the corners. Turn the canvas edges to the wrong side, folding close to the stitches, so no canvas shows. Sew canvas in place along 3 sides, leaving buckle end unstitched. To attach buckle, see diagram below.

To begin and end strands

To begin, hold an inch of yarn on the wrong side of the piece and work stitches over this end. All other strands are begun and ended by running them under the stitches on the wrong side of the piece.

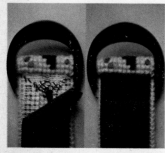

Slip-stitch backing to the wrong side of the belt, leaving 8cm (3″) unstitched along sides at buckle end. Place buckle over end and fold end over bar 2.5cm (1″). Sew end securely and slip-stitch backing in place, covering stitching at end.

Cross-stitch

Cross-stitch is a counted thread stitch and can therefore be used on both canvas and even-weave fabrics. The technique is the same. The stitch has two steps: the first is an understitch worked diagonally and the second is a stitch worked diagonally in the opposite direction over the first stitch to form a cross. Cross-stitch can be worked to any size, over two, three, or more threads, but must always be worked over the same number of threads both vertically and horizontally so that a perfect cross is formed. Make all crosses touch by working adjacent stitches in the same hole of the fabric or canvas. When cross-stitch is properly

Individual crosses

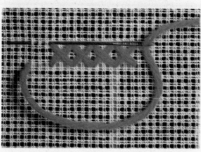

1 Bring needle out at bottom left of cross. Insert needle at top right and bring it out at top left.

2 Insert needle at bottom right of this cross and bring it out at lower left of the next cross to the left.

3 The reverse side is two horizontal lines with double stitches at the bottom.

Horizontal row

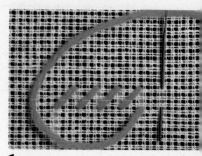

1 Bring needle out at bottom left of row. Insert needle at top right; bring it out at bottom right of each cross.

2 Bring needle out at bottom right of row. Insert needle at top left; bring it out at bottom left of each cross.

3 The reverse side is a row of double vertical stitches.

ked it is not necessary to turn
piece to follow the line of a
gn or to take the threads across
e areas on the reverse side. The
ret of easy, neat working lies in
wing how to stitch horizontally,
ically, and diagonally.

examples shown here should
read from top to bottom – the
d picture shows how the stitch
look on the reverse side if it
been properly worked. The
mples show how to work hori-

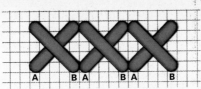

zontally, vertically up, and diagonally down. By turning the page
upside down and working the steps
from bottom to top as they then
appear, you will also be able to
work cross-stitch vertically down

and diagonally up (left and right).
It is important to see that the
thread which lies on top of the
cross always slants in the same
direction. (See the diagram above
where thread B lies over thread A.)

ertically up

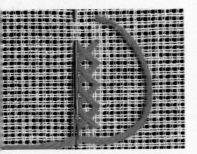

Bring needle out at top right of
s. Insert needle at bottom left and
g it out at top left.

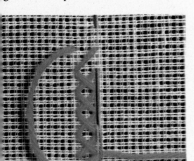

Insert needle at bottom right of
s cross and bring it out at the top
ht of the next cross above.

The reverse side is two vertical
es with double stitches at the left.

Diagonally right

1 Bring needle out at bottom left of
cross. Insert needle at top right and
bring it out at top left.

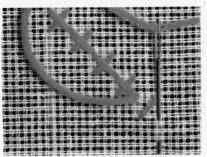

2 Insert needle at bottom right of this
cross and bring it out at bottom left of
cross diagonally down to right.

3 The reverse side is a diagonal line
of stitches at right angles.

Diagonally left

1 Bring needle out at bottom left of
cross. Insert needle at top right and
bring it out at top left.

2 Insert needle at bottom right of this
cross and bring it out at bottom left of
cross diagonally down to left.

3 The reverse is a line of horizontal
and longer diagonal stitches.

How-to

Small motifs for cross-stitch

Fashion magic with embroidery

Cross-stitch is an attractive and easy way to add pattern and color to plain fashions and accessories.

Cross-stitch can be worked on any even-weave fabric by counting the threads, and on checked fabric by using the checks as a guide.

To embroider on uneven-weave or fine fabrics, work the crosses over a piece of canvas basted to the fabric.

Sprinkle lucky four-leaf clovers down the sleeves of a favorite shirt. Work a pretty bouquet of country flowers on a pocket. Or, wear a lively little girl on your sleeve.

Working cross-stitch

Work a sample on a scrap of fabric to determine the number of strands of embroidery cotton to use. Be sure all crosses touch.

On even-weave fabrics: Count the threads of the fabric and work the crosses over the same number of threads horizontally and vertically.

Over canvas: Baste cross-stitch canvas or soft, single-thread canvas to the fabric, being careful to make the threads of the canvas parallel to the threads of the fabric. Embroider the design by working over the threads of the canvas and through the fabric. Do not catch the canvas with the needle. When the design is finished, remove the basting threads. Cut excess canvas away from the design, then draw out the remaining canvas threads with tweezers, leaving the cross-stitch design on the fabric.

Nine small motifs

Here are hearts for your collar, stars for your cuffs,
a butterfly for your belt, and other exciting
small motifs to enliven your clothes and accessories.

ountry garden bouquet

is charming spray of flowers is equally effective in
oss-stitch on place mats and tablecloths or as a
corative design on a plain-colored knitted pullover.

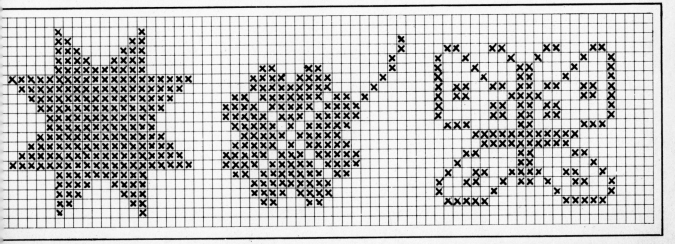

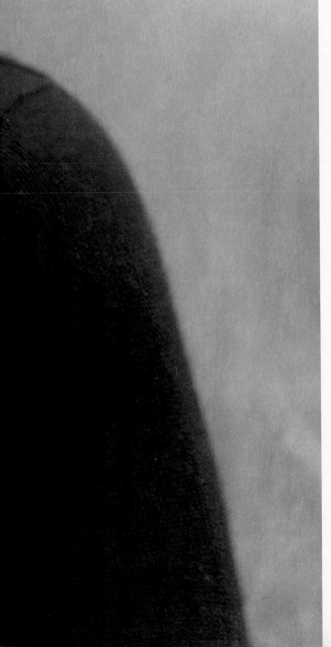

The knitted stitches are covered with embroidery worked in tapestry yarn.

Knitted-in look with embroidery

A pullover in stocking or stockinette stitch can be embroidered with a motif so that it looks as though it were knitted in. Quickly worked, the embroidery will transform an ordinary pullover into a personalized one.

Use the cross-stitch chart to embroider the pretty blossom motif onto a plain pullover. Each cross on the chart represents one embroidery stitch on the pullover and each embroidery stitch is worked over one knitted stitch of the pullover.

The chart can also be used to work ordinary cross-stitch on an even-weave fabric such as a tablecloth, mats, or cushions. For most pullovers, except those worked in very fine wool, the best type of yarn to use for the embroidery is tapestry yarn. On the dark pullover illustrated, the blossoms are worked in glowing autumn colors—red, orange, and gold, with olive green leaves. If you find the complete motif too large, pick out a single bloom with a few leaves. A smaller design is more suitable for larger

bust sizes. The design can also be used effectively on the edging of a pullover, around the neck, or in a random pattern on one or both sleeves.

The chart also shows a Greek key pattern border which has many decorative uses. Work it in cross-stitch around the edge of a tablecloth or a cushion, or on knitted garments in the same way as the blossoms. Try embroidering the border vertically onto a pullover from shoulder to hip or down the middle of the sleeves. To save time, you will find it much quicker to work each stitch of the border over two knitted stitches in height. This will make the pattern appear narrower and more open, as the knitted stitches will not be fully covered by the embroidery wool.

Swiss darning or duplicate stitch

Knitting a design into a piece is slow work. With this stitch, you can add the design to pieces worked in stocking or stockinette stitch after it is finished. The stitch is particularly effective for large, bold motifs on a plain background.

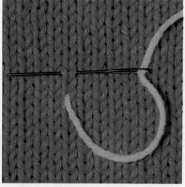

1 Bring the needle out at the base of a stitch and then insert it behind the next stitch above, from right to left.

2 Pull the needle through and insert it again at the base of the same stitch. Bring it out at the base of next stitch to the left.

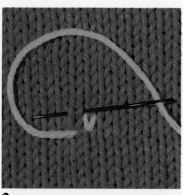

3 To make the second stitch, insert the needle behind the next stitch above and pull the yarn through as before.

4 Vertically from top to bottom: Insert the needle in the base of the stitch and bring it out at the base of stitch in the row below.

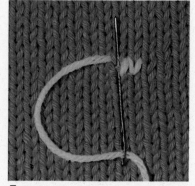

5 Vertically from bottom to top: Insert needle in base of stitch and bring it out at the base of the stitch in the row above.

6 Diagonally down from right to left: Insert needle in base of stitch and bring it out in the stitch diagonally down to left.

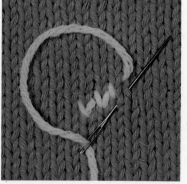

7 Diagonally up from left to right: Insert needle in base of stitch and bring it out in the stitch diagonally up to the right.

8 It is important, when embroidering knitted items, to avoid carrying the threads across large spaces between color areas on the reverse side of the work.
The embroidery yarn should not be thinner than the yarn on which it is worked so that it will cover the stitches of the knitting. Embroidery stitches must never be pulled too tight.

Ideal for cushions, tablecloths, bedspreads, blouses, and much more

Here is the blossom motif which was worked on the pullover, shown in different colors and as a cross-stitch design. The motif is given on the chart; each square represents one cross-stitch.

As cross-stitch is a counted thread stitch, it is simplest to work on an even-weave fabric. The size of the finished motif depends on the number of threads to 2.5 cm (1") and the number of threads over which the cross-stitches are worked. A bold motif would look striking on a linen tablecloth, or cushions around the home, and simply stunning on the back of a shawl. A small motif would look charming on table mats, or even a delicate blouse.

If you want to embroider the design on a fine or uneven-weave fabric, baste a piece of soft canvas to the fabric and work over the threads of the canvas, following the chart in the same way. When the motif is complete, cut away the excess canvas and pull out the threads with tweezers. The Greek key design, also given on the chart, is an unusual border for any household linen.

Decorative embroidery can be

As simple as ABC

Here's an easy chain-stitch alphabet —
just right for initials and
monograms. Trace these embroidered
letters for actual-size patterns.

EFGH

MNO

STUV

Z

The Personal Touch

The charm of hand-embroidered initials will give clothes and accessories an individual look.

Delightful on children's clothes

Bright decoration on denim casuals

An embroidered tie for a special gift

A T-shirt with a touch of chic

A sporty letter for your favorite cap

Eye-catching jean embroidery

Personalized table linen for special occasions

New life for an old handbag

Chain stitch

Chain stitch is one of the oldest embroidery stitches – and one of the most versatile. It can be worked in single rows for outlining, in blocks of rows as a filling stitch, or as a detached stitch cluster for a pretty daisy motif. Chain stitch is often used for working monograms and initials because its flexibility is ideal for embroidering along the curved lines of the letters. There are several chain stitch variations and the detached chain stitch or the lazy daisy stitch is shown here.

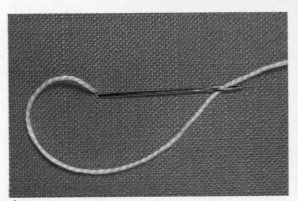

1 Work from right to left. Bring needle up through fabric and hold thread in a loop with your thumb. Reinsert needle at the point where it emerged.

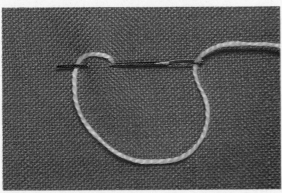

2 Bring needle point out a short distance away. Thread lies under needle point. When the needle and thread are pulled through, the chain is made.

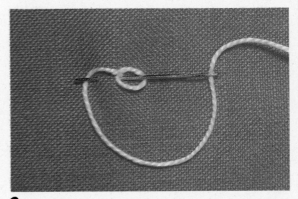

3 To make another chain stitch, reinsert needle at point where it emerged, bringing it out again the same distance away as for previous stitch.

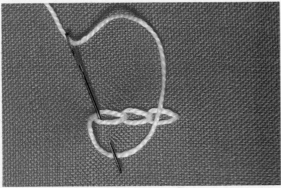

4 To change direction, bring the needle point out in the new direction and continue working chain stitches in the same way as for a horizontal line.

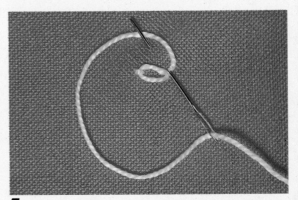

5 To make detached chain or lazy daisy stitch, make a chain and secure it with a tiny stitch. For round flower, work a circle of detached chains with a common base.

Party table settings

Ice crystals and stars

Decorate a linen table runner with ice crystals in three shades of blue. Group motifs as shown and work two rows of chain stitch for the border.

A single motif and chain stitch border will enhance a breakfast set.

Marking design on fabric

The ice crystal motif at left is actual size. Trace the motif onto transparent paper and transfer it to fabric with dressmaker's tracing paper in a contrasting color. Place the dressmaker's tracing paper face down on the right side of the fabric. Place traced motif on top and, holding both firmly in position, go over the lines of the design with a pencil or a dry ball-point pen. Use a single motif or arrange motifs in a group. Trace the motif as many times as required. The lines will be covered with embroidery and will not show.

Embroidering the motif

Use pearl cotton or three strands of stranded embroidery cotton. Work the straight lines of the design in chain stitch and the petal shapes in lazy daisy stitch.

The star pattern gives five different star sizes. Trace each outline separately.

Marking design on fabric

Trace stars and mark them on fabric as for ice crystal embroidery. The tablecloth illustrated here has a wide band of stars embroidered across the center. The motifs could also be grouped in a wide border for a circular cloth or as a large central motif. A pretty effect could also be achieved by sprinkling the stars at random all over the cloth.

Embroidering the stars

Use pearl cotton or three strands of stranded embroidery cotton. Choose four or five colors in the yellow to bronze range. Work each ·star outline with two rows of chain stitch. The first is worked on the design line and the second outside it.

Pressing embroidery

Place embroidered piece face down on a well-padded surface and press with a steam iron or a dry iron and a damp cloth. Work from the center outward and press lightly so the stitching will not be flattened. Remember that pressing is not ironing. Raise and lower the iron with a gentle motion. Press in direction of the grain.

A milky way of stars in glowing golds and bronzes or a crisp pattern of ice crystals in frosty blues to embroider in simple chain stitch.

Tablecloth for Christmas
In festive flower motifs

This bold poinsettia motif in red and green create an impressive tablecloth for festive occasions. Using the actual-size patterns, table linens can be designed in a number of ways by arranging the flower motifs in different patterns and combina-

tions of sizes. You migh use the large motif in th center of a tablecloth with other large flower in diagonal lines to th corners. A band of larg flowers could be worke along a table runner or o a place mat, while th small motifs would mak

Stem stitch

Stem stitch is an outlining stitch and is used for both straight and curved lines. It can also be used as a filling stitch and it is suitable for all kinds of fabrics. Two variations of the stem stitch are shown here.

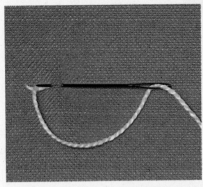

2 Insert needle a short distance away on pattern line and bring out next to the previous stitch.

Simple stem stitch

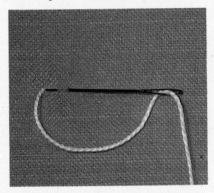

1 Bring thread through fabric. Insert needle on pattern line and bring out halfway back on line.

3 Continue to work from left to right along the pattern line, always keeping thread below needle.

Cable stitch or alternating stem stitch

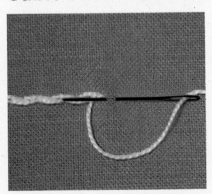

1 Work the first stitch as for the simple stem stitch, holding the thread below the needle.

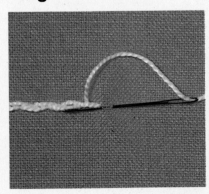

2 Work the second stitch with the thread above the needle. Continue, alternating the thread position.

Red and green are the colors of Christmas, but beautiful poinsettia motifs are timeless. Work them in a rich color scheme or all in white, using simple stem stitch.

pretty all-over pattern r a decorative border. Work small flowers on apkins for a matching et. Transfer the pattern o the fabric and work the otifs in stem stitch with tranded cotton or pearl otton in rich traditional hristmas colors.

Poinsettias

Simple blossoms in
two sizes for
Christmas decorating.

Felt Advent calendar

Easy enough to make in a weekend!

The five bright motifs are ironed onto
the felt with bonding net,
so the only stitching is around the pockets.
This is quick and fun appliqué!

Materials Required: Felt: .6 m x 160 cm wide and .1 m x 90 cm wide ($\frac{5}{8}$ yd x 0″ wide and $1\frac{1}{4}$ yds x 36″ wide) for background and pockets. Pieces of felt for motifs. Iron-on interfacing: 8 x 82 cm (19″ x $32\frac{1}{4}$″). Packet of bonding net. 2 wooden rods for hanging.

Making the calendar
Cut out the background piece to measure 54 x 88 cm (21″ x $34\frac{1}{2}$″). As felt shrinks, it is wise to iron it with a damp cloth before cutting out. Iron the interfacing onto the back of the felt, leaving a 3 cm ($1\frac{1}{4}$″) border all around.

Pockets: Cut 4 strips 8 x 45 cm ($3\frac{1}{8}$″ x $17\frac{1}{2}$″), 3 pieces 8 x 9 cm ($3\frac{1}{8}$″ x $3\frac{1}{2}$″), 1 piece 20 x 23 cm ($7\frac{7}{8}$″ x 9″). Mark off the strips at 9 cm ($3\frac{1}{2}$″) intervals. Appliqué a motif on each pocket. Stitch on the pockets: the top center pocket is 14 cm (5$\frac{1}{2}$″) from the top edge and 23 cm (9″) from each side. Stitch 1 pocket side close to the pocket edge. The pocket is pleated, so push the excess to the center and stitch the other side. At the

base, make a $\frac{1}{2}$ cm ($\frac{1}{4}$″) pleat on each side and stitch across. Attach the strips in the same way, beginning 7 cm (3″) from the side edges. Add the 2 small pockets and 1 large pocket at the bottom. Turn the 3 cm ($1\frac{1}{4}$″) seam allowance to the back and stitch it down with bonding net. Turn under 6 cm ($2\frac{1}{2}$″) at top and bottom of the felt. Iron down 3 cm ($1\frac{1}{4}$″) at the outer edge with bonding net, leaving room to insert the rods. The calendar is now ready to hang on the wall. Fill pockets with gifts for each day up to Christmas Eve.

All the motifs are given actual size so that they are easy to trace.

Even more motifs given actual s
to trace onto the adhesive fab
and appliqué in felt.

Appliqué-
with bonding net

Adhesive iron-on bonding net sticks two pieces
of fabric together so that sewing becomes
superfluous. It is backed by a special paper
on which you can draw or trace the appliqué motifs.

How-to

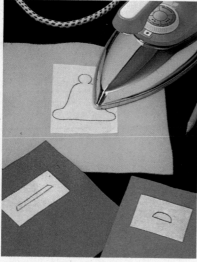

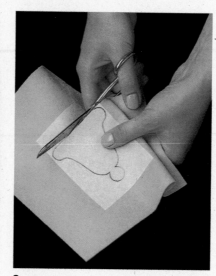

1 Draw the motif on the paper
side and cut out roughly. Place the
adhesive side on the wrong side of
fabric and press for 2–4 seconds.

2 Cut out the motif with a pair of
sharp scissors. Take great care to
cut around the curves and corners
as accurately as possible.

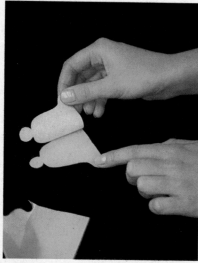

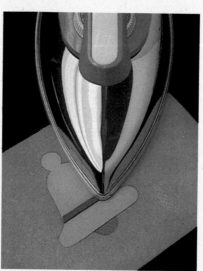

3 Allow to cool completely for
about 1 minute, then peel off the
paper carefully. A film of adhesive
will be left on the fabric.

4 Press the motif onto the background, then press with a damp
cloth on the wrong side for 10
seconds. Test after 10 minutes.

Rugmaking with a latch hook is an easy craft to learn and an absorbing way to make a strong, good-looking rug with a rich pile. Here is a clever motif which can be arranged and rearranged in dozens of different rug designs!

Something new to try in rugmaking

A geometric puzzle rug

Try sixteen squares laid in the same direction.

Turn two rows to create a different pattern.

Four squares turned to the center make a circle.

Alternating squares make four wavy diagonals.

Waves run across the rug at the top and bottom.

Turn all the squares and it's different again!

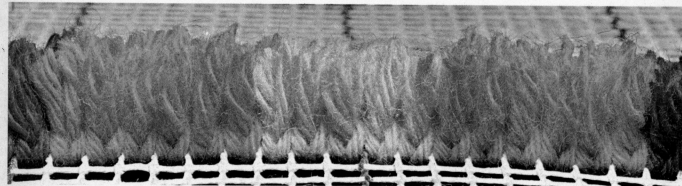

The yarn is knotted into every mesh of the canvas, working from left to right across each row. Since the yarn pieces are all the same length, a lush, even pile is achieved.

The fun of having a puzzle rug never ends. If you get tired of your design, you can simply rearrange the motifs. Or, try a complete change by assembling the motifs so the rug is a completely different size and shape. Make a runner for a hall two squares wide and eight squares long or a hearth rug three squares wide and five, six, or seven squares long.

Size: Using 3½ mesh per 2.5 cm (1″), each motif will be 39.5 cm (15½″) square and a 16-square rug will be 158 cm (62″) square. Using 4 mesh per 2.5 cm (1″), each motif will be 32.5 cm (12¾″) square and a 16-square rug will be 130 cm (51″) square.

Materials (for each motif): Rug canvas: 44.5 cm (17½″) square of 3⅓-mesh canvas or 38 cm (15″) square of 4-mesh canvas. Pre-cut rug yarn: 4 packs dark red, 2 packs brown, 2 packs pink, 1 pack yellow. Latch hook. Rug binding. Carpet thread. Upholsterer's needle.

Estimating yarn amounts

The number of strands in pre-cut packs varies with the brand. We used packs containing 320 pieces per pack. To determine the number of packs required, count the squares of the chart to determine the number of pieces of each color required. Multiply each number by the number of motifs you plan to make, then divide by 320 or the number of pieces in your packs to determine the number of packs needed to complete a large rug. Our 16-square rug requires: 68 packs dark red, 28 packs brown, 25 packs pink, 10 packs yellow.

Planning the design

Decide the size and shape of rug you need and then draw your rug design on paper, arranging the motifs in a way which pleases you. Based on the number of motifs you have used for your design, determine the yarn and canvas needed.

Working the squares

Cut canvas to the proper size, always making sure there are 51 holes across and 51 rows, plus a 1″ margin all around. Begin working at the lower left corner of the canvas, 1″ in from each edge. Follow the chart at left to work design (each square represents 1 knot on the canvas). Work across rows rather than working color areas to achieve even blending and avoid separation of pile into color areas.

Joining rug pieces

Trim away excess canvas at the corners of each square. Turn canvas margins to the back and sew in place. The squares are joined by the diagonal basting stitch used for flat-joining in dressmaking. Place two squares side by side, pile side down. Using curved upholsterer's needle and carpet thread, sew squares together, matching meshes. Following your design sketch, join the squares in strips, then sew the strips together to complete the rug. Sew rug binding over the joinings and around the edges. When the rug is finished, run your hand in one direction over the pile to remove any loose fibers. Trim any uneven ends.

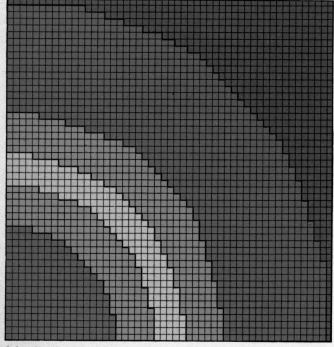

Color chart for the puzzle rug motif. Each square represents one knot. Begin at the lower left corner and follow the chart row by row.

4-movement Smyrna knot

Deep-pile rugs can be made by knotting short lengths of rug yarn into a canvas base with a latch hook (also called latchet hook). The Smyrna knot can be made in two ways – the 4-movement and 5-movement methods. The 4-movement knot, which is shown here, is quicker to work than the 5-movement knot.

These two knots create pile which lies in opposite directions. When two people are working on the rug at the same time (one at each end), by using both methods, the pile will all lie in the same direction when the knots meet in the middle of the canvas. The 5-movement knot is explained in another rug feature.

1 Rug yarn for making latch hook rugs can be bought in packs, pre-cut and ready to use.

2 Fold the yarn in half and loop it around the shank of the latch hook, holding the ends together. Insert the hook into a hole, under the horizontal threads, then push it out through the hole above. The yarn is below the horizontal threads.

3 Turn the hook slightly and pull the yarn ends across the open latch. Draw the hook back through the canvas. This will close the latch and pull the yarn ends through the loop. Be careful not to split the yarn with the latch when it closes.

4 Tighten the knot by pulling the ends. (The knot will be easier to make if you keep the yarn very loose while working and tighten it after you have finished). Work knots from left to right across each horizontal row, following illustrations 2–5.

5 For an evenly knotted rug, work completely across canvas before beginning next row. Work design by following color chart (each square represents a knot on the canvas). Place a few strands of yarn in each color close at hand. This will speed up the pace of your work.

Alternative color schemes for the puzzle rug

Color requirements vary according to the style of the furniture and the amount of light in the room.

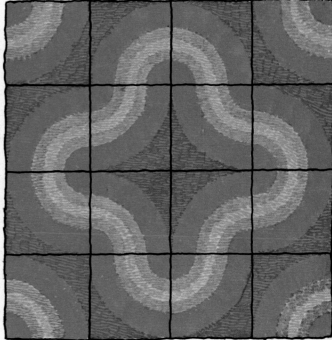

This is the scheme shown on the previous pages. Warm colors go well with transparent materials such as plastic and glass.

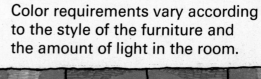

For rooms which need a touch of coolness, choose colors in the blue to green range. Lime green will sharpen up the softer tones.

Yellow gives a feeling of warmth and light to a sunless room. Modern wood furniture goes well with yellow hues.

Rich green and brown, plus a singing red, complement antique furniture and brass and copper accessories.

A hard-wearing rug of braided sisal

Sisal is a strong, natural fiber which can be used to make bold rugs for country flooring.

A braided sisal rug is ideal as a doormat – it's colorful and hard-wearing.

Here's a new craft to try!

Braided sisal in the round

Sisal braiding is easy — even children can do it — and here is a fascinating way of using sisal to make attractive rugs and mats. Lengths of sisal are first braided and then twisted and stitched into flat rounds. Finally, the rounds are stitched together to make decorative patterns.

Sisal is a practical material for making rugs. It is extremely hard-wearing, and easy to clean, as the finished structure of a braided rug is rather open and dirt falls right through. This makes them ideal for hallways, children's rooms, and places where the foot traffic is likely to be heavy. Braided sisal can also be used to create beautiful table mats and covers. Hot plates won't harm the table and, after a meal, the mat is simply shaken to remove food fragments. Give free rein to your

Rounds can be stitched into a formal arrangement for a stunning hearth rug.

3-strand braiding

The technique is illustrated with pairs of strands in three colors so you can see where to place the strands. The rug rounds were braided in a single color, but tri-color rounds could certainly be used to produce a tweed. Note: It is important to keep the tension even.

Making the rounds

Six strands of 2-ply sisal were used to make the rounds for the rugs. Sisal is available in natural and a range of attractive colors. Cut the strands approximately $1\frac{1}{3}$ times the length of the required braid. A 30″ braid will make a round 9 cm (3½″) in diameter. A 60″ braid makes a 12.5 cm (5″) diameter round and a 90″ braid makes 15 cm (6″) diameter round.

creativity when planning the designs. Sisal can be obtained in bright colors but if you find that only the natural sisal is available, dye it to the color you require. Follow the manufacturer's instructions.

Planning the design

Before starting to braid, draw a plan of the rug or mat on squared paper, indicating the colors to be used. Each circle must touch adjacent circles so that the sisal rounds can be stitched together.

Making a rug or mat

Make the rounds, laying them out according to your pattern. Stitch rounds together as shown at right.

Braiding and stitching sisal rounds

Knot three pairs of strands (2 red, 2 green, and 2 white) at one end and hang them from a hook. Place red pair to the right, green pair in the middle, and the white pair to the left.

2 Holding the red pair in your right hand and white pair in your left, bring the red pair to the middle over the green, being careful to keep the strands flat (do not let them twist).

3 Bring the white pair to the middle over the red. Continue to braid in this way by bringing outside strands from alternate sides to the middle. Knot or bind the braid at the end.

Cut lengths of sisal and knot them together at one end. Holding the strands by all the ends, dampen the strands in water to make them more pliable. Do not dampen ends.

2 Bind the cut ends of the sisal with tape. This not only prevents fraying, but makes the strands easier to handle. The tape can be easily removed when the braiding has been completed.

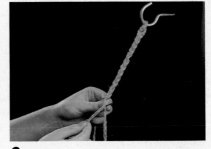

3 Hang the knotted strands from a hook while braiding as this helps to achieve an even tension. If a hook is not available, the knot can be shut in a drawer to secure it.

4 At about 10 cm (4″) from the end, cut away one strand of each pair to reduce the bulk of the braid. Continue to braid with three single strands. Tie ends with a cut-off strand.

5 Starting from the tied-off end, bend the braid into a round and begin to stitch the braid to itself, using a heavy-duty thread. Use flat joining stitch and stitch on the wrong side of the work.

6 Work in a circle, making sure that the stitches are not pulled too tightly so that the round will not become distorted.

About 5 cm (2″) from the end of the braid, turn the knotted end toward the center of the round on the wrong side and cut it off straight across.

Stitch down the raw ends on the wrong side, making sure that no stitches show on the right side of the round.

Variations on a theme

The color scheme is up to you

Play up the design with warm shades of red, pink, gold, orange, and brown.

You can be the proud owner of beautiful rugs like these. Adapt the colors to your decor, or even better, design your own rug so that it will be exactly the size and color you need.

Use neutral colors to tie in with a more traditional mood. Add life to the scheme with a rich crimson and a sunny yellow.

Color your canvas in cooler tones to create a totally different effect with the same design of zigzag and straight lines.

You'll find that it is great fun to design your own rug, so why not let the whole family get involved? Give everyone sheets of squared paper and some colored pens or pencils — you can work out the general color scheme ahead of time. It is probably easiest to begin with a geometric design, but after a while, you will become accustomed to working with curved lines on the squared paper and you can make representational shapes such as fish or flowers.

Designing is much easier than you think. The important thing is to have fun with it and let your imagination run free. You'll be surprised by the results.

Designing a rug

First, determine the shape and size of the rug you wish to make.

Draw this outline on your graph paper. Each square of the graph paper represents one horizontal bar of the canvas and there is one knot per horizontal bar. Fill in the outline with your design, making sure the size and shape of the design are appropriate for the size and shape of the rug.

Transferring a design

Cover a large, flat surface with several layers of newspaper and place the canvas on top. Being sure to leave 5 cm (2″) margins on each side, transfer the design with waterproof paints or marking pens as shown at right. Be sure to let the paint or ink dry thoroughly before starting to knot.

5-movement Smyrna knot

This is the reverse of the 4-movement knot. By using both, rows worked from opposite ends will lie in the same direction

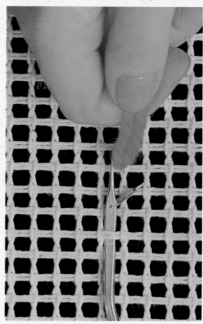

1 Insert the hook under the threads of the canvas. Open the latch and slip a piece of rug yarn onto the hook.

2 Hold the yarn ends even. Pull the hook back through the canvas until the yarn is halfway through the hole

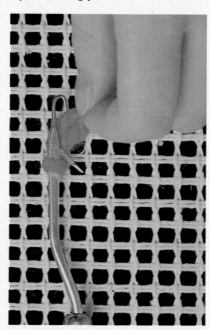

3 Push the hook back through the loop until the latch is above the loop and open. Turn the hook slightly so the latch is more toward you.

4 Pull the yarn across the hook and pull the hook down. The latch will close and pull the ends through the loop. Pull the knot tight.

Designing, Painting the canvas

Work out your own design on graph paper –
you may be impressed with your artistic ability.

Smyrna knots are worked on $3\frac{1}{3}$ or 4 meshes to 2.5 cm
(1") double-thread canvas. The horizontal threads are
held in place by the twisted vertical threads.

2 Thick rug wool is used with this canvas. The yarn
can be bought in ready-cut packs or bundles and it is
available in a wide range of colors.

Work out your design
on graph paper with felt-
tipped pens.

4 Transfer your design to
the canvas with waterproof
paints or markers.

Each square of the graph represents one knot on the
canvas. Be careful to transfer the design to the canvas
so that the color is clearly marked on every mesh.

6 Work knots into each mesh across the row, with yarn
which corresponds in color to the painted canvas. Watch
the design come to life as you fill in the colors.

It is easy to design a pattern on graph paper

Here are just a few designs – you will think of dozens more!

Working a design

Leaving a 5 cm (2″) margin all around, cut away any excess canvas. Place the canvas on a flat working surface and weight the far end if necessary. Fold margin of the end closest to you to the back.

Begin at the lower left corner and work the knots through both layers of the canvas. Work a complete row before beginning the next one.

At the other end, fold back the margin and work through both layers as at the beginning. Turn in the raw edges at the sides and stitch in place. Cover the raw edges with rug binding.

When working on a large rug, two people can work on the rug at the same time if one starts at one end with the 4-movement knot and the other works at the opposite end with the 5-movement Smyrna knot. When the two ends meet, the pile will be lying in the same direction along the entire rug.

ZIGZAG RUG

Size: On 3¼ mesh canvas: 80 x 120 cm (30″ x 47½″). On 4 mesh canvas: 66 x 99 cm (26″ x 39″).

Our rugs are 104 knots wide and 157 knots long. The outer border is 5 knots deep and the inner contrasting border is 8 rows deep.

Amounts of yarn required:

Natural color scheme:
20 packs brown
24 packs beige
8 packs olive green
7 packs white
8 packs crimson
8 packs rust
4 packs yellow

Red and orange color scheme:
9 packs gold
7 packs bright red
9 packs white
11 packs orange
11 packs pink
24 packs dark red
19 packs brown

Blue and red color scheme:
17 packs turquoise
24 packs dark blue
9 packs red
7 packs pale blue
11 packs light blue
15 packs medium blue
6 packs pink

Index

Index

Notes

Notes

Notes